HAUNTED
MARYSVILLE,
MONTANA

Thank you, Gibbs Towing (Mr. G himself?)
for the interruption & getting my ℞ front shoe
back up to pressure after 2 weeks search!
(Yep... Supposed to be self-reliant. Working on it!)
VM Vince Monorek Sept. 1, 2022
22 Ten Mile / Ashland, Montana

Say, is there an air hose
around?

SURE! If Mr. Gibbs isn't
available, y'got Lame Deer...
...Broadus... hey,
even Forsyth!

M 9/1/22

Marysville, circa 2019. *Author photos.*

HAUNTED
MARYSVILLE, MONTANA

VINCE MORAVEK

Haunted
America

Published by Haunted America
A Division of The History Press
Charleston, SC
www.historypress.com

Copyright © 2020 by Vince A. Moravek
All rights reserved

Back cover, top: Town icon Betsy the Jalopy cruises through another high Rockies winter; *inset*: Marysville Methodist Church, 1886. *Both by Ginny Thomas, mountainmaam@mt.net/406-443-0545.*

First published 2020

Manufactured in the United States

ISBN 9781467145480

Library of Congress Control Number: 2019956056

Dedicated to

Andy and Samwise Phillips, Marysville's Heavy Metal Heroes and without whom I'd have been lost years ago.

As well as

All the great people of Marysville past, present and future.
Thank you. In all my years and miles, this is the first true community I've found.

CONTENTS

A BOOMING LITTLE PLACE

Marysville owes its existence to the nearby Drumlummon Mine developed by a determined miner named Tommy Cruse. The British-owned Montana Mining Company acquired the mine in 1883. Expansion of Drumlummon operations, including a large ore processing mill, brought miners, their families, and businesses to the adjacent camp called Marysville. Soon substantial wood-frame and brick buildings replaced the old camp's log shacks. Within a few years Marysville consisted of genteel residences surrounding a vibrant commercial district. Along with grocery stores, hotels, mercantiles and restaurants, Marysville included churches, a variety of fraternal societies, an orchestra, and a substantial schoolhouse. A brewery and 27 saloons satisfied the town's earthier needs. One writer predicted in 1892 that "within a dozen years Helena will only be a suburb of Marysville." It was not to be. By 1895, a severe national depression and the mining company's legal woes drifted Marysville into a slow decline. A fire devastated the commercial district in 1910 and the Northern Pacific Railway abandoned its line to Marysville in 1925 as the ore, and business, played out. While not quite the "Denver of the North," the town endures and is proud of its heritage.

"A Booming Little Place." *Author photo.*

MARYSVILLE MONTANA

IN 1870 THE MINING TOWN OF MARYSVILLE WAS ESTABLISHED AND NAMED FOR THE FIRST PIONEER WOMAN HERE MARY RALSTON BY THOMAS CRUSE OWNER OF THE FAMOUS DRUM LUMMON MINE

BY 1900 THE MARYSVILLE MINING DISTRICT WAS REPORTED TO BE THE RICHEST GOLD MINING AREA IN THE WORLD WITH A PRODUCTION OF $ 60,000,000 ONE-HALF OF WHICH WAS TAKEN FROM THE DRUM LUMMON MINE

OTHER LOCAL RICH GOLD MINES ALSO PRODUCING AT THAT TIME WERE THE BALD MOUNTAIN BALD BUTTE EMPIRE BELMONT PENOBSCOT GLOSTER AND SHANNON

THE TOWNS POPULATION AT ITS PEAK WAS ESTIMATED TO BE 4000 RESIDENTS THEY HAD THE SERVICE OF TWO RAILROADS AND 60 BUSINESS ESTABLISHMENTS INCLUDING 2 NEWSPAPERS

ERECTED BY THE MARYSVILLE PIONEERS ASSOCIATION-1970

Marysville historic sign, from 1970 Marysville Pioneers Association. *Author photo.*

ACKNOWLEDGEMENTS

WITH SPECIAL SALUTES TO:
Ginny and Moris Thomas
Ellen Baumler
Terry Beaver
Chris and Rebecca Boyles
Editor Artie Crisp and the fantastic Arcadia/History Press staff
Brian Hammerschmidt and Amanda Grimmett
Harry McGee
Marilyn Melton, Princess Jasmine and Leroy
The Orsello family
Steve and Vanessa Soboyna
Richard and Jen Sparrow of Sparrow Enterprises

WITH ADDITIONAL KUDOS TO:
Gary and Ann Baker
Dave Felton
Chris Coyle and Krissy Gillespie
Ron and Peg Herman
Staff of Marysville House
Marysville Pioneer Society
Debbie Peterson
Don Sherman
Troy Shockley and KCAP
Every other deserving person or soul whose names I've unjustly spaced on.

Acknowledgements

AND FINALLY, SOME WONDERFUL TOWN DOGS:
Hank (Mayor), Tuff, TJ, Bella, Leroy, Princess Jasmine, Cooper (x2), Bear, Boots and Buckles.

Medium Michael Sweet passed away on February 10, 2019. We were honored by one of your last investigations and hope you now embrace the answers we yet seek.

INTRODUCTION

I stumbled into Marysville by accident.

I had lingered in tiny East Glacier after a project, and when forced to return to the Helena area, I feared the prospect of the chaotic big city as much as I resented leaving the adventures and daily marvels that come with residing on the edge of Glacier National Park. Rental prices were way out of my range. But the Fates didn't let me down. After striking out with all other options, a single email changed my life forever: an offer to rent an empty house in this high-mountain ghost town that had been vacant and on the market for several years. "The Bunkhouse" was indeed an old dorm for miners, needed tons of work and was cosmetically trashed. Normally, they wouldn't consider renting it, but hey, if I didn't mind...

That allowed some of the most amazing experiences of my life.

I felt I had moved into a living museum exhibit of the Old West mining past. Although 90 percent of the infrastructure is gone, abandoned ruins still outnumber modern homes. Each day brought a new dawning awareness of the near-indescribable scope of the pioneer metropolis crammed in this tiny bowl and throughout the surrounding hills. The Marysville District's leading role in many ways exceeds the other better-known Montana tourist ghost towns yet is overlooked because it survives as a living town.

This new stranger encountered friendly waves from day one. I was admittedly unprepared for the winter but never suspected I looked pitiful enough to find cords of cut firewood magically appear in the yard. Same

Ruins above Main Street with Betsy. *Author photo.*

Cabin ruin interior. *Author photo.*

with boxes of extra cold-weather gear and groceries on my porch. Now that I know everybody, I see that was a community taking care of its own; several neighbors were responsible, and not one sought recognition or payment. This single bachelor received anonymous Christmas presents and Easter baskets for the first time in decades. When my main car blew its engine and I was stuck with a big 1979 Lincoln backup, a neighbor was so appalled at my winter travel struggles that he bought me a surprise AWD Subaru! Yes, a payback deal, but that's just partially reflective of this stunning community. Friends wonder if I'm being groomed for some mysterious purpose and will one night wake up to a yard full of townsfolk in black robes and burning torches. But no. Reality rules. Along with unprecedented graciousness, I *have* managed to annoy, repulse and anger my usual share. Hopefully I can keep that percentage low in this unique place.

I discovered a new adopted hometown filled with amazing people surrounded by interesting areas to explore. Wildlife abounds. Moose have wandered in at times, along with free-range cattle and escaped pet donkeys. Our mayor, Hank, is a fang-grinning malamute. With all the routine cool weirdness, who could suspect the biggest surprises lay in wait?

Abandoned in place. *Author photo.*

I'd heard the usual passing rumors, but ghosts or supernatural events were the last things on my mind when I had a mind-blowing paranormal double-feature late one night in my second rental house. Shocking as that was, it was only the start of a real-life *series* of spooky events that played out over the next weeks like a favorite *Twilight Zone* episode. Forevermore, I *know* "something's going on" beyond our reckoning. That also started the questions.

So I invite you up into the high Rockies of south-central Montana, to Marysville and the Marysville Mining District, for the first glimpse into its vast untold reports of ghosts and other supernatural events (GSE), all with a spectacular background legacy of sometimes unbelievable, usually unappreciated historical figures and other impressive personalities. This is no grocery list of old stories. You'll join an active quest as you help fit the many puzzle pieces of rumor into a wondrous—and chilling—panorama of secrets and surprises.

But knowing what I know now…um, allow me to let *you* go first.

CHAPTER 1

THE HAUNTING OF JULIAN HOUSE

Did you know this was one of the more haunted houses in town?
—Ginny Thomas, 2016

THINGS THAT GO SMASH IN THE NIGHT

Had I just witnessed a miracle?

In the fall of 2016, I overcame what any sane person would see as an insurmountable challenge: finding another affordable rental house in Marysville. Especially one with the unbelievable timing of becoming available the same week the old house sold and I'd been handed my walking papers. Better yet, the new digs were right up the street! I'd been saved from the certain doom of attempting to find and afford a new rental and then remain sane in busy Helena after years in small towns like East Glacier Park and Marysville.

Divine intervention or careful what you wish for?

"Did you know this is one of the more haunted houses in town?"

This cheerful revelation came from a trusted neighbor as I hauled stuff up the street. Ginny Thomas is absolutely credible and only reported what she'd heard. "Loud bangs and other noises in the middle of the night. So much so that [the current owner living in Missouri] had to have a Native American shaman perform a sage ceremony to banish them. There's also supposed to be some creepy mirror in which people saw strange things."

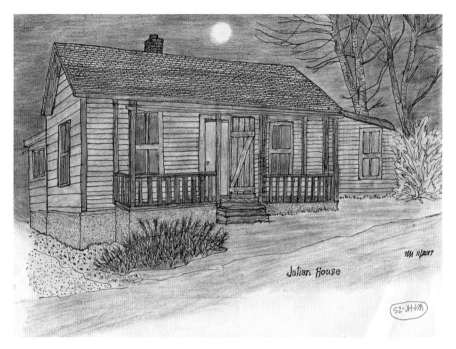

The moon over Julian House. *Author sketch.*

Hmm, *that* wasn't in the brochure.

Actually, there *wasn't* any brochure. The only reason I had the house was due to the fantastic Marysville townsfolk. No pitchforks or torches showed up my first year, and after two years, the newcomer must have passed some kind of acceptance threshold. Those who saw my predicament got together, vetting me to their mutual friend the landlord. I moved in sight unseen (except, of course, for the outside), caring for nothing more than getting it.

Did I care that its original street-facing porch and 1890s structure was a perfect stand-in for Jed Clampett's cabin? Not with the entire back half completely renovated like a Hyatt Regency suite. And its further odd amalgam of modern renovation versus pioneer original only added to the charm. A dark dogleg hall led off the kitchen—modern site for a washer/dryer but part of the original structure. Layers of old wallpaper were peeling off to reveal the 1894 *Helena Herald* "pioneer insulation" newspaper pages still plastered tight against hand-hewn log walls. Even June Cleaver would find the patterns of the remaining patchwork linoleum floor quaint and outdated.

Entering what I called the Dark Hall was to step into the past, from the 1940s back through to the 1890s. A trio of ominous narrow doors shut off other ancient unused rooms: a low woodshed, a tiny old bathroom choked with dust-covered 1930s-era fixtures and a bedroom-sized chamber, also with original walls and scattered odd personal items abandoned decades ago. A 1924 edition of *Grit*. A leather belt aged hard and brittle. Old cooking utensils hung on nails, rusty tools and a pile of 1920s–'30s newspapers stacked neatly on a dusty table. A March 1936 edition carried an interesting piece on the hunt for outlaw gangster John Dillinger after his latest jailbreak.

The big adjoining living room was the main part of the original cabin, but taken together, it was like having a modern home with half a haunted house tacked on. Complete with the aforementioned "creepy mirror."

Unremarkable at first glance.

Rectangular. Foot and a half tall. Shade over two feet long. Mounted in a simple faded green wooden frame, jammed high up on an old shelf in the Dark Hall. Reflections were muted behind decades of old soot, grease spots, dead flies, dust, spiderwebs and hanging cobwebs. Simple thing but yep, creepy all right. Especially with the stories.

The scoop from multiple sources—including the owner, himself a personal witness—was that multiple strange bright lights would appear, moving about within the mirror without any reflective source in the outside world. Same confirmations on the loud unexplained night sounds. But no worries—all quiet since the sage ceremony.

In fact, the previous residing couple had no disturbances whatsoever. Of course, there was that *one* time when the stereo burst on by itself in the middle of the night, but that might have been a timer malfunction—despite never using the feature. But certainly no loud noises or phantom mirror lights. Did they avoid the Dark Hall by night just like I found myself doing?

Should I dig deeper, or did I even *want* to know more at this point?

"If I do, it's only for historical interest and always with respect!" I giddily announced aloud that first week, not really believing I was addressing anything more than my own superstitions, although let's cover all the bases, ha-ha—*huh?*

Two seconds after my declaration to the Dark Hall, a very distinct metallic *TINK!* sounded in the (personally dubbed) Roaring Twenties Room. Subtle but with the clarity of a ten-penny nail dropping. Hardly a bang or crash, yet something seemed to fall on cue. Room clutter held no revelations besides my own worked-up imagination.

And no moonlight horrors erupted other than my snores.

New digs for the unwary with Princess Jasmine on the porch. *Author photo.*

At least for the first three months.

January 30. The depths of a dark, frozen night when I woke out of a dead sleep. Felt and looked like 3:00 a.m. or damn close enough—no clock was checked. I was sleeping on the sofa in the new part of the house beside the kitchen with a clear view into the old section up front.

Nothing but black silence. What woke me up? Usually I slept like granite, waking at times, sure, but typically back out in moments. It was unprecedented to even get to the point of opening my eyes to look around. Somehow this time I did, noting the two guest dogs I was hosting for a neighbor were also awake. Neither showed any sign of alarm, yet both had their heads up, necks turned for mild looks into the kitchen.

Utter peace. Confusing. Until the Attack of the Poltergeist.

CRASH is but a mild definition of the metallic/porcelain/dining utensil/ small appliance bashing clatter that then exploded out of the kitchen. Not a single smash but more an *avalanche* of domestic kitchen items. Exactly, go figure, as if that tall but shaky item-loaded metal shelf stand in the corner just toppled over. Either that or a skinny, top-heavy lamp I insisted on placing atop the microwave fell over again, this time taking toaster, coffeemaker, cups, saucers, breadbox, several dishes and a couple fully loaded metal toolboxes along with it. If it was a spooky movie special effect, Steven Spielberg would have approved wholeheartedly with wide grin and happy clapping.

What did I do in this stunning encounter of the paranormal?

In an equally remarkable demonstration of how a groggy brain operates—or perhaps *fails to*—my reaction was nothing more than a disgusted grunt and sneering grumble, absolutely certain it was my own carelessness to blame. I had a unique skill to set things up for later falls. Not one thought of the supernatural. The dogs cringed at the sudden noise but otherwise lay watching.

Aw, I'd check out the mess in the morning.

I barely began turning over when another burst of disturbance hit, this next one fierce enough to vibrate sofa cushions. Think of an extremely irate Dwayne Johnson suddenly appearing in your front room, taking a running kick to a major brace beam while releasing double armloads of rough-cut lumber to scatter, smashing against the nearest interior walls.

Criminy! Whatta ripple effect! Really outdid myself this time!

Snore.

I WOKE UP ANNOYED but glad I waited for morning to confront both the mess and my new lengths in bookshelf overload, poor kitchen furniture choice and/or whatever home decorating Rube Goldberg time bomb I'd managed to set up for myself.

Instead, I confronted the inexplicable.

You guessed it: absolutely nothing was out of place.

Insert here a whole morning of investigation/attempted debunk. Include several neighbors' inspections and inevitable shrugs. This was right after a brief thaw as well: metal roof, noted clear all around and specifically examined the afternoon before. Undisturbed old snowpack everywhere else below roof lines. No tree branches or debris. Not one steaming jet engine embedded in the roof after falling off a passing C-130 or carcasses of forty-pound squirrels. Etc., etc. Add to that the difference between confidently hearing things *inside* versus *outside.*

No dream. The best evidence for me is my utter bonehead reaction, not even cluing into the old reports in the middle of their demonstration.

Bright daylight beyond the self-deprecation brought mostly awe. *Wow! Did that REALLY happen? YES!* Kind of exciting too. Despite a long and firm personal conviction that encountering a true spook would trigger instant screamin' retreat, it was thrilling to consider I had witnessed *two* probable supernatural events. I might have been too ignorant to recognize it at the time, but at least it allowed me to hang around for them both without freaking out. To say nothing of quite likely getting scared out of my residence that very night never to return—a real possibility *had* my central nervous system been more engaged.

So what next?

I made excited reports to calm, nodding neighbors. The owner happened to call that very morning on an unrelated matter and was able to confirm that what I heard was pretty much the same thing that frightened previous tenants. Far out!

One problem before claiming absolute proof: my long distinguished record of being unutterably wrong. Occam's Razor ruled my overflows of active imagination into the real world; namely that all things being equal, the simplest explanation is the most likely. Yet at the same time let's not forget "absence of evidence is not necessarily evidence of absence."

Physics still rule our planet. Some mechanism had either **A**: produced audio bursts mimicking domestic destruction powerful enough to shake the floor or **B**: violently flung about a variety of heavy objects and then, conveniently, silently levitated all objects back into their exact starting points cleaner than a clandestine FBI office search.

Or **C**: I was missing something. Which option feels most likely?

Bottom line: just because I couldn't find a natural explanation doesn't mean there wasn't one. And this coming from the Kansas transplant (with plenty of acute-care medical experience, I might add) who mistook the low-frequency drumbeat of mating grouse for symptoms of a terminal aortic aneurysm and once called in a big cloud as a wildfire. Better be careful.

Unless the noises recurred and were able to be documented, it would remain just another tale, no matter how excitably I told it. Blank stares from the dogs when asked for collaboration. Nothing else to do but wait and keep camcorder handy.

Or, if I dared, take a closer look at that creepy mirror.

SECRETS OF THE DARK HALL

I got up the courage after an anxious week of calm silence.

Sixty-watt light bulbs are my strict conservative limit, but there's a brilliant hundred-watt exception burning in the Dark Hall's single outlet. My reflection could barely be made out through the dirt, grime, insect smears and overhanging cobwebs on the mirror's surface. Several minutes of deep study showed nothing but the need to replace my current razor.

It was probably a dubious investigation technique—my face could compete with the scariest of phantoms. Frankly disappointed at the quiet nights, I was ready for a new thrill (not *too* extreme, mind!) and felt prepared to encounter ghost lights in a mirror. I needed to move it into the front rooms where stray fireflies might catch an eye, as it sure wasn't going to happen in the Dark Hall. *That* remained daylight-use only.

A whisk broom and Windex got rid of the worst of the dirty film accumulated over who knows how many years. The bottom of the frame had been thickly painted onto the shelf; a razor was required to free its bottom section. The mirror itself was tilted forward at the top, long ago pushed firmly against the hall's low ceiling planks, and was solidly jammed.

Dang heavy thing! I could only shift it side to side before eventually sliding it to one side off the shelf. When it finally scraped away, I had to brace against its unexpected weight as a cache of dust-caked letters, old envelopes and other stashed papers fluttered out in a sooty cloud.

Except for a single letter addressed to the "Mrs.," all envelopes were addressed to David A. Julian of Marysville. Here's a specific list:

- A mess of disintegrated paper that could be anything. Recognizable is an old brochure for V-belts (top half dissolved) and an intact (1930s-era) four-page booklet of instructions on the correct application of SHU-SOLE shoe repair cement. (Zanol Products, New York, Cincinnati and Paris).
- Three-page Comparative Consolidated Statement of Income and Comparative Balance Sheet of the American Power & Light Company located in New York. For the year September 1930–September 1931. Envelope with one-cent stamp and New York postmark.
- One-page letter handwritten in ink to Delia from Anna. Dated January 9, 1940. Addressed to Mrs. David A. Julian (Marysville), return address Mrs. Anna Julian, 846 5th Avenue in Helena. Postmarked Helena, January 10, 1940. No stamp, envelope torn and right-side section absent. This simple letter is most striking to me as it makes the people so real. Anna enclosed a check for $6.50 for the kindness of bailing out "Edd" at the poolroom. Using standard inflation rates, $6.50 is the equivalent of $116.59 in 2019 dollars. Perhaps

scandalous—a century ago. Now it just emphasizes these were real people with real lives; and none could guess I'd be gawking at their personal business almost eighty years later. Anna writes how she mailed it after expecting a visit that didn't occur, that everybody was quite well, she was keeping busy with work and "the store is still up for sale." A final line states an enclosed clipping was from the *Helena Record-Herald*, but there was no clipping found.

- Typed 8x10 business letter to Mr. D.A. Julian on letterhead from S. Hamilton of the Butte Machinery Company, Aluminum and Arizona Streets, Butte. (*Mine Operators Machinery Stored Free of Charge!*) November 8, 1929. A few polite paragraphs acknowledging previous correspondence and accepting a bid for the removal of "lumber in place" and scrap iron at Lane Mills.

- Two thin Statement of Accounts (D.A. Julian) from Helena's Central Market that used to exist at 112 Broadway (*Wm Gieseker, Prop. Wholesale and Retail Dealer in Fresh and Salted Meats, Poultry, Fish, Butter, Eggs, Etc. Phone 79*). Date stamped March 30, 1937. The single 3/18 unspecified entry indicates $0.80. The second

A school group with a young David Julian, presumed to be the boy standing on the left next to the man. *Marysville Pioneer Society.*

is date stamped May 6, 1937. Three handwritten entries of "4/21, 24" and "29" total up to $5.18. Crude pencil sketches below suggest rough plans for some kind of V-shaped bracing structure.

- A pair of Central Market receipts. March 18, 1937, showed a purchase of 1⅓ pound of hamburger for 25 cents and a 55-cent rib roast. On March 24, 1937, Mr. Julian bought another rib roast for a buck twenty and a pound and a half of burger for 30 cents.

- A small blue return envelope for Cook Sporting Goods. Col. 1601 Larimer Street, Denver, Colorado. (*Our 60th Anniversary!*) A great picture of the big three-story brick store bears no resemblance to the modern skyscraper Google Maps shows in its place.

- Handwritten (pencil) letter dated January 2, 1930. Just a few polite sentences from Mr. D.A. Julian to the county treasurer (Lewis and Clark County) asking if any outstanding taxes exist on "Mrs. Denolda Shaffer's waterworks." A penciled note below from Jos. Oker, Co. Treas. (January 23, 1930) relates yes, and $7.77 would take care of it if paid that month. County treasurer printed envelope (left side torn off) addressed D.A. Julian. Two-cent red Washington stamp canceled and postmarked June 3, 1930.

- Typed letter (D.A. Julian) dated December 28, 1929, on the letterhead of the Freemason's Ottawa Lodge here in Marysville. Chass H. Hull, secretary, was congratulating Mr. Julian that at the previous night's meeting David was "duly elected to receive the degrees of Masonry" and was invited to do so on their next meeting of January 10. Printed Ottawa Lodge No. 51 envelope, right side torn off, but December 29, 1930 Marysville postmark survives (this was at a time the town *had* a post office, of course).

- A thick, brittle-at-edges folded-up paper turned out to be a three-by-two-foot schematic map of (at least portions of) *Underground Workings at the Gould* [mine], *Graball vein*. The Gould was a local thriving mine a century ago. No date, lettering printed but obviously by hand in flourishing Old West style. Blue like a blueprint, tunnels, labels all white. Eye-catching piece for a wall but otherwise lacking any drama or apparent significance. Certainly no "treasure buried HERE!" notations.

A rare group shot highlighting several members of the Julian family. Suspicions are high that "Unidentified #9" (*back row, second from left, next to Anna with large hat*) may be revealed as another family member on the shape of the nose alone. What do you think? *Marysville Pioneer Society.*

- Final mystery: a torn-off envelope flap, folded tight and stained with dark blotches below a scrawl of heavy pencil. The handwritten script was so rough it required examination from several other people before the odd, faintly menacing message became clear (revealed later). Without context, it was virtually meaningless.

No glittering hidden gold, but having the names of the past residents—possibly the first ones in the house—was invaluable in its own right. I might have obtained this information from neighbors in the know if I ever thought of asking, and later, with the family name now specifically identified, they did become great resources. I then hit the Net for specifics.

The David A. "Arthur" Julian subject of the letters is technically David Julian Jr., son of David A. Julian Sr. Grandparents were Louis (Lewis) E. and Anna M. Julian, storekeepers who emigrated from Sweden in 1880. Somehow the Julians made their way to Montana and set up a mercantile in Silver City, the old pioneer town six miles down the valley. By the 1900 census, the Julians were listed as living in Marysville with five children: Oli, Annie, Nellie, David and Edward. By that time, Mr. Julian was running a local grocery and/or mercantile.

Sadly, that family list came from daughter Nellie's obituary. She died on May 14, 1905, of diphtheria at the tragic age of twelve. She was laid to rest in the Marysville cemetery before the family moved her to Helena's Forestvale Cemetery in 1931.

If a ghostly energy truly was involved, could Nellie be the source? A tragic death on premises is the standard prerequisite for hauntings, right?

But it likely isn't Nellie. That's because neighbor testimony told of an older cabin/house nearby—that later burned down—that was the original pioneer home and likely Nellie's residence at the time of her death. However, other indications suggest the cabin *was* located on the property; at any rate, the Julian family eventually took up residence on site. The letters are to Lewis's grandson, dates from 1929 to 1940, possibly the third generation to live in the same home in which I now resided.

From neighbors' misty memories to completely subjective gut feelings— Nellie's story seemed too convenient and the violent manifestations somehow uncharacteristic of what I'd expect from a little girl's spirit—I dismissed Nellie as a likely responsible ghost. Hers was indeed a life cut tragically short, but she had lived long enough to embrace the love of her family and, eventually, was moved to rest among them in Forestvale.

Identifying another supernatural "suspect" was probably impossible.

According to research, by the 1950s or '60s, all of the remaining Julian clan had moved to Helena. The bloodline continues on strong with many grand/great-grandchildren, but (far as I can tell) the Julian name of that specific family has passed into the great legacy of our pioneer West.

Who might have lived here from the mid-1960s through the late '90s is unknown. There are no murders or other drama on Internet searches. In fact, a cemetery list recorded the vital stats on each member of the local Julians: dates of birth, death, cause, ages and the city in which they passed. Except for Nellie, those later generations appeared to live into their seventies and eighties—a respectable lifespan for most, with "natural causes" the usual note at the end. All passed away in Helena. The single exception was a mysterious blank entry from the last generation: *Rex*, listed only as passing away in the 1960s at the age of eighteen. All else was blank.

I later found a neighbor who had gone to high school with Rex. Harry McGee wasn't a close friend but recalled that, unlike most kids of the time,

Rex had a car. He drove it like a hot rod, in one opinion. "Used to zoom around all over…would dust up these big donuts in the school's parking lot." Perhaps prophetically, Mr. McGee stated his strong belief that Rex had died in some kind of "pretty bad" auto accident.

Another family tragedy never to take lightly, but in this context eliminated as the last documented possibility of an on-site death.

REALITY CHECK. TIME TO dismiss that growing fantasy of ghostly night bangs deliberately leading me like some hack Indiana Jones to a hidden cache of pioneer secrets that shockingly reveal…um, not much of anything besides the incredible value of rib roast in 1937.

Great plot while it lasted and quite interesting to get this far. Ghost of a Julian reaching out from the grave to get someone to find this dubious treasure and…what? It sure delivered a lot of personal appreciation, and even old grocery receipts were an awesome and humbling glimpse into the past. But it was just the equivalent of a time capsule stuffed with nothing but Walmart receipts.

Well, not that lame. Although of general interest, the letters and other papers are unique and valid artifacts of history. Perhaps invaluable treasures for descendants. The night noises did not repeat; there was no activity suggesting rage at the trespass nor acknowledgement of the find. The creepy mirror sat in a chair in the kitchen, collecting fresh dust without a hint of the slightest sparks.

The whole thing was just weird karma or simple random coincidence. There goes my chance to dial up Zak Bagans. The next logical step was to return the documents to any family I could find—not an easy task. I had some names but no contacts. Net searches and random calls from the phone book failed.

A week later, the "stash" became just another stack of kitchen clutter. I still intended to scope out any Julian descendants, but that thought was far from my mind when neighbor Marilyn Melton (in an odd twist, the owner of the dogs I'd been watching that night) called to check if all was well. My house looked unoccupied during that week's snowstorm, and I had been staying at a friend's home down the mountain.

I appreciated the call—and then recall struck of something Marilyn had mentioned long before I moved into Julian House: how her best friend used to live in that "old green house" up the hill. The green house in which I now lived. And the friend turned out be (let's call her "Ms. Z," as I did not clarify use of her real name) the granddaughter (I believe) I thought might still be out there but was unable to track down.

"Oh yes, we talk all the time. She lives in Helena. Why?"

Logistics prevented a personal exchange, so I simply arranged to turn the papers over to Marilyn to hold for her friend's next visit. I secured them in a big protective Ziploc for the short four-block walk—with one spooky detour. I ducked into the garage to retrieve my sunglasses out of the car. I had turned and began walking back out when, for some unknown reason, my attention fell on a single flat wooden plank leaning between wall studs out of a jackstraw clutter of other boards and lumber.

There were no ghostly whispers or phantom shoulder taps. No glimpses of shadow, light or *any* other sensory manifestation that attracted attention. What happened next, however, was undeniable: with the mindless reflex of putting the cap back on a tube of toothpaste, I stopped, crouched down and grabbed the small wooden plank. I turned it over to see this stamped in Old West script:

L.E. JULIAN
SILVER CITY, MONT

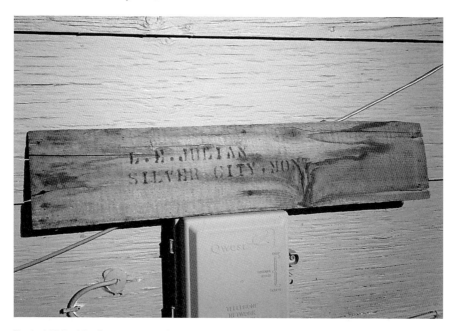

Early 1880s shipping crate panel from Julian patriarch Lewis's Silver City mercantile. It was declared by the family as the most treasured relic of all recovered. *Author-with-trembling-hands photo.*

The letters and other papers were indeed considered important to the family. According to Marilyn, Ms. Z was "over the moon" to receive them. Especially that simple wooden plank, cracked with stained nail holes, likely the single surviving piece of a shipping crate from the Julians' Silver City store—a great family artifact dating back to Lewis and Anna's first arrival in the 1880s.

This final *Hey, buddy! Forgot something!* stamped crate incident freaked me out. I can't decide if it was better or worse that there *wasn't* a skeletal hand pointing the way or clear spiritual possession. I plucked it up as if snagging car keys on the way out the door, with zero conscious consideration of any kind. An example of our demonstrably smarter subconscious? I'd seen it when first moving in (forget those years of undisturbed cobwebs and dust or the simple fact that only a small unmarked end was poking out)…my brain remembered it…riiiight?

Now *that's* scary.

And a final shock was still lurking.

DAYS PASSED. THE CREEPY mirror got relegated to a forgotten corner of the front room; just something else to trip over. Ms. Z allowed me to keep the old advertisements, map piece and other unrelated fragments. Included was that ripped envelope flap with the scrawled pencil. Message or nonsense, it defied translation. However, after later sharp-eyed analysis by others, the scribble revealed itself like a 3-D puzzle. Although scoured letters loop in a frenzy, once they are recognized, that's all you can see and it becomes clear:

nobodys [sic] *sweetheart now*

Definitely a bigger score on the Creep Meter than a dusty mirror. As ominous, sinister…or utterly meaningless as one chooses. It fits, perhaps, if there had been some documented murder where a guy busted in on his cheat'n girlfriend or—no, a young man spurned his honey, she came calling with a machete and—

Who knew? Who *could* know at this point? Great fodder for imagination, but zip for hard data or actual documented history. Barely strange enough to keep a small thread of spooky streak humming and perhaps, just maybe, hang onto in case there's more to the story. Somewhere. *Somewhen.*

Mystery lasted less than seventy-two hours. Then Ms. Z called and shook me to the core.

Nobodys sweetheart now: the cryptic message of the hidden cache behind the infamous "haunted mirror." *Author photo.*

Of course that wasn't her intent. It was a gracious thank-you for the return of the letters and other materials. Although I was always conscious of limiting my snooping, Ms. Z spoke so openly about her family—and did not laugh at the circumstances of discovering those papers—that I delicately asked about "Rex," the one blank line in the history. I instantly regretted it when hearing her wistful reply, strong now but still reminiscent of loss. Thankfully, she expressed no problem or reluctance at the truth.

Rex was her brother, and as street rumor suggested, a car wreck had claimed his life.

So he died in the hospital or out on a highway somewhere. Stop snooping into this nice lady's past pain and shut up!

One last unexplained item: the weird note. I hurried on, grateful to change the subject but trying to be delicate. Its author could have been male or female. I deliberately didn't speak the message, just mentioned that there was an odd scribbled note and the general opinion that it might suggest someone was having, as I put it, "romantic trouble."

The subject had not been changed after all.

"Well, Rex suffered some terrible chest injuries in that accident," Ms. Z. continued. "He was really involved with this girl at the time and felt he was so banged up that he could never anymore be anybody's sweetheart.

"That's why he shot himself."

Rex did not pass in a hospital or out on some lonely road. He killed himself at home. At Julian House.

ANALYSIS AND DISCUSSION: SPIRITS AT REST?

Later at a summer picnic, Ms. Z was able to examine the note in person. She was calmly accepting of any possibilities but had no confirmation, knowledge or firm opinion whether it was related to Rex in the least. If her ultimate shrugging disinterest was feigned, it was an Academy Award performance. She allowed me to keep the envelope with the concerned reluctance of tossing a candy bar wrapper.

About as meaningful?

I wasn't so sure.

Why bother to stash it away? (Okay, I hear you…same question for old market receipts and a 1931 instruction brochure on the use of **SHU-SOLE** shoe repair. *None Genuine Without Our Trade Mark "Zanol"!*)

Suicide note? Rex's final statement of distress? Are the brown stains blood? Did this last declaration, sad and useless as it may be, nonetheless represent something Rex *wanted* to be heard? Any traditional ghost story would say *yes*, classic plot. This note was hidden away by whomever first found the body. A decision was made that there was no need to add to the family's (or girlfriend's) distress by having it revealed. Hiding it may certainly have been an act of good intention in terrible circumstances yet one that kept an unsettled spirit from having his last words heard and finding peace. Cue loud nighttime detonations to get attention, lead 'em the next logical

Left: Art Julian, David Julian's son, at reunion picnic, circa 1970s. *Marysville Pioneer Society.*

Right: Samuel Franklin Ralston Jr., the son of Marysville namesake Mary Ralston, went on to become superintendent of Glacier National Park (1914–17) and later a state senator. *Marysville Pioneer Society.*

step to a mirror that manifested storms of attention-seeking lights trying to point out the messages hidden behind.

If life (or *afterlife* in this case) imitated fiction and that's what happened here, then great. There were other forces at work but all worked out, no pun intended, in the end. Spirit's happy, stuff gets back into the rightful family hands and all is quiet on the Western Front. The only feeling now is a lingering disappointment (much mitigated at night) that if there *was* any story behind the haunting of Julian House, this was the final chapter.

The house sold soon thereafter, and I moved out after six peaceful months that followed.

Talk about things ending not with a bang but with a sigh.

At least JoBeth Williams didn't have to mud-wrestle a single reanimated corpse.

CHAPTER 2

PHANTOMS OF THE RED HOUSE

The details were clear in spite of the entire figure being transparent....

Could this cozy, fairly modern home I was staring at really be the infamous haunted "Red House" I had heard so much about? The location matched even if the rightful name was confusing; some insisted it was really called the Pink House, while others scoffed, declaring pink a later mistake only after its early red paint faded under years of hot summer suns and brutal Rocky Mountain winters. It didn't help that the house had been recently repainted again in modern times—this time in a completely different color, far from any shade of red whatsoever.

I refrain from clarifying the exact house color or location after having the opportunity to meet the current occupants over a Marysville House beer—nice folk reporting nothing but peace in their quiet home. (Good for them but...*rats!*) the man of the house was twenty years younger than me and about a foot taller. Therefore, it didn't take much clairvoyance to prophesize a high chance of getting pounded into the ground like a fencepost if I made the mistake of triggering any unwanted public attention. At any rate, the house's appearance isn't as important as the startling—and scary—events that have taken place there.

The Red House remains a charming cottage in its declining years—so much so that a few previous tenants from yesteryear feel no reason to move on. *Author photo.*

THE ELEGANT LADY

There's no doubt that full-figure apparitions top the list of most intriguing GSE phenomena. (GSE—shorthand for ghosts and other supernatural events—embraces the full range of everything a reasonable person may perceive as "spooky" or "supernatural" with likely paranormal origins.) It should come as no surprise that one of these also topped the local ghost stories. Nor that traveling to the willing witness was about a forty-yard commute across the dirt street across from Julian House to an even older—and much cooler—vintage home pieced together from pioneer cabins. Some say it's the oldest occupied structure in Marysville.

Harry McGee is another in-the-know native resident (as well as artist, awesome military vet and master metalsmith responsible for the fanciful Western scenes crowning Maryville's street signs). Others have confirmed his details and suggested that over the years, he is not the first nor last to have an encounter with the Elegant Lady of the Red House.

Harry woke on a dark night to notice a faint shimmering glow in what should have been a pitch-black living room. Something about its strange character made Harry take special notice, studying it while silently slipping out of bed. What was out there? There were no cable boxes or electronics, nothing with LEDs. *Shimmering* yes, but without the alarming reddish glow of a smoldering fire. He smelled nothing burning.

Flashlight of a burglar? Another dreadful possibility dismissed after a second's consideration. The fairy glow was extremely clear in the dark room but diffused—moving to be sure, but with a slow deliberateness in a single direction.

Harry crept to the open doorway, abruptly deciding to go no farther.

At least not while the pale glowing form of a ghost crossed through the living room.

No horrible Charles Dickens chain-rattling nightmare here. The apparition was that of a young or early middle-aged woman, hair done up in a tasteful style and dressed in old-time formal attire. The details were clear in spite of the entire figure being transparent. Harry was able to see through her to the faintly illuminated corners of furniture visible on her other side.

Marysville townsfolk group. *Marysville Pioneer Society.*

High lace collar. Moving with a back-straight, finishing school posture that emphasized a girdled waist and frilly bodice. Although her glittering dress faded away below knee level, she moved through the darkness with the graceful glide of a practiced hostess.

Harry reports watching "with a full side view" as the apparition slowly crossed the room. He remembers being rightly shocked, wide-eyed and freaked out. A little scared as well, but remarkably not as much as might be expected. That was because the ghost did not seem menacing in any way. There was a level of fright in its very nature, yet Harry sensed no threat or hostility. A spirit not of great past tragedy but powerful past...*hospitality?*

Years later on the sunny summer front porch of a different house altogether, Harry wishes—just a little—that he had tried to speak to the Elegant Lady before she vanished against the far wall. The sense of graceful hospitality was that strong Then again, maybe refraining from doing so was a good thing. The librarian scene from the opening minutes of *Ghostbusters* comes to mind. Maybe Harry had been thinking of the same shocker of a beautiful ghost instantly transforming into a screaming demon hag once you attract its attention.

Or maybe Harry was thinking of something different altogether. Something that happened in real life, not the movies. An experience that was about as terrifyingly far from warm hospitality as you can get.

ATTACK IN THE NIGHT

The man who faced one of my worst nightmares definitely remains anonymous. I'll call him Gus. And Gus would rather everybody forget all about it, forever. Especially, I bet, ranking right below me, *himself.* But dismissing such a shocking experience is impossible to completely stamp out of the local collective memory—or elude the grasp of a local snoop of sufficient prying annoyance. History had already written him in.

The principal witness and his family were not interviewed. I didn't even ask, following the stern advice of several people who warned me not to bother. I got the known "common knowledge" story from multiple sources, all with consistent basic details, but there would be no witness quotes or personal insights. For Gus, described as not just a skeptic but a total unbeliever in ghosts, spirits and other so-called supernatural claptrap, GSEs simply do not exist.

Which made it all the more disturbing for him.

IT WAS THE REQUISITE dark, scary night. Gus was sleeping on the sofa in the living room of the Red House. The timeframe is iffy. I believe he was the only one in residence, sometime after Harry had moved out. It seems as if half of Marysville has played musical chairs with the limited homes in town at one time or another.

He woke from a deep sleep—but not from a vague sense of presence or unease but from the flat-out sudden and unprovoked attack of a powerful unseen force that wasted no time in pouncing on a reclined Gus. The sensation of being held down has been reported in many ghost stories around the world, but the report here exceeded the standard in the raw, brutal intensity of this experience. It was no "sensation" but a full-on surprise assault of tremendous power. The many descriptions make it sound akin to waking up to the knee of an enraged meth-crazed linebacker on your chest.

Take my word on seeing Gus in person. A friendly neighbor yes, but one who currently holds high position in my Top Ten People Not to Ever Tick Off. His mind and body have been built and seasoned from a lifetime of Montana out-of-doors work and recreation. He is not a lightweight dude. Nevertheless, Gus had to fight with all his strength against the heavy weight pressing down on his upper body, limbs and chest, not so much holding him down but apparently intent on shoving him straight down through the cushions to smother in the wreckage of the collapsing sofa.

Worst of all were the tight, squeezing grips of phantom talon hands it's told Gus could feel clamped on both his forearms. The squeezing force behind these were as bad as the blunt weight pressing down on his chest. His neck was now starting to painfully bend against the thinly upholstered armrest, thrashing uselessly against an overwhelming power as his face started to get shoved aside into the backrest and—

The invisible force winked away with the speed of a flicked switch, a velocity almost surpassed by the alacrity with which Gus got the hell out of the Red House, never to return.

At least at night.

WHEN IT COMES TO personal paradigms to Gus, flying elephants would be as easy to accept as phantom all-star wrestlers. Nevertheless, he did find himself in desperate battle with...*something*...unseen, inexplicable and utterly strong. According to sources, Gus willingly conceded that if it had been a real wrestling match, he'd have heard the ref declaring victory for his opponent. Whatever it was, he fought hard against it—felt

Blacksmith shop of Drumlummon Mine. *Marysville Pioneer Society.*

its overwhelming power. He knows better than anybody that it wasn't a waking dream or hypocognic hallucination.

But for those who accept the possibility, there is supporting evidence for a GSE. Strong, down-to-earth, no-nonsense men don't make a habit of making up stories or speaking about unexplainable experiences that, if not for the powerful impact he could not hide from those close to him, would never be spoken of or admitted.

If it was a spirit of the Red House, it hardly fits the descriptions of—or impressions of—the Elegant Lady. Should ghost behavior truly reflect their living selves, then perhaps another presence resides there. For if a ghost is a true surviving personality, how likely is it for that graceful hostess to resort to such barbaric strong-arm tactics on her guests? Harry did not report the lady sporting oversized biceps or any MOM tattoos.

Perhaps Gus had put his stocking feet up on the coffee table earlier that evening, failed to use a coaster for his beer or unwittingly committed some other Gloria Vanderbilt transgression. Whether living residents are aware of her or not, it seems that formal social graces are still demanded by the lingering Elegant Lady of the Red House.

Unless her gliding spirit is not alone.

ANALYSIS AND DISCUSSION

If it is truly haunted, how many ghosts are in the Red House?

The two events here don't jive with the superficial elements: a vaporous image of a gracious hostess one time; a fierce, invisible, hostile poltergeist or outright demonic entity the next. This may lend credence to my overall GSE theory that they may take many forms as a result of many separate mechanisms, some of them natural. They are both supernatural, but each exists apart as separate "things"—mindless image echoes versus active, real-time, frightfully interactive forces. Like pineapples and cherries are both wildly different fruit.

Accepting the theory that powerful emotions or mind states can somehow get recorded, later to result in apparitional replays, then perhaps the Elegant Lady is nothing more than that, some unknown but perfectly natural "instant replay" of a past powerful atmosphere or emotion. In obvious answer to the old adage, trees falling in the forest without witness certainly make noise. But it may be that these replay apparitions require the presence—the energy and senses of a living person—to activate, perceive and power their little scene.

But an effervescent 3-D recording doesn't have the presence, power or stupendous mechanical energy necessary to overwhelm the strength of a strong adult man in the middle of a full-out, adrenaline-fueled struggle over a short but respectable time period. In consideration of the evidence, other dark forces may exist there than a dainty ghost recording.

AFTER MY OWN EXPERIENCES in the Julian House, I began asking about local haunts purely out of personal curiosity, unfortunately before recognizing that their sheer number and startling scope rated formal research and documentation. Confirming details from multiple sources, including personal testimony from Harry, tells me these last two accounts are 100 percent truthful without tall-tale elaboration. But to the best of my recall, the Red House kept coming up beyond the two experiences just offered. I have nothing specific in scribbled notes, just that there was a significant amount of activity throughout the years. This is mentioned only for full fairness in my interpretation of the site's possible level of GSE occurrences. Without at least two confirming sources, a number of "I heard of" GSE phenomena supposed to have also taken place at the Red House cannot be authoritatively included here.

Yet.

The Red House's infamous local reputation suggests far more spooky events than can be confirmed today. Is it true that Harry wasn't the only one to encounter the female apparition, that there was another modern-day sighting of the Elegant Lady but this one was so disturbing to the unknown witness that he or she adamantly refuses to speak or even acknowledge the incident? One rumor claims a female spirit is headless.

It's highly likely the Red House holds other startling secrets.

CHAPTER 3

A MORNING OF MURDER AND MAYHEM

My God, help me! She's trying to kill the whole family!
—John Wright Allen, October 29, 1896

384 GRAND STREET—"THE BUNKHOUSE," 2015

Marysville mornings were the picture of small-town peace and quiet. Except, go figure, for the occasional phantom gunshots and explosive detonations. I had only been a few months in residence before getting startled right out of my chair by a pair of sharp firecracker *pops* followed close behind by a singular heavy explosion. It sounded like someone took a couple potshots at a propane tank with spectacular results.

Even from inside the well-insulated 1901 house, I could tell whatever it was had occurred uncomfortably close. As in a block or two, surely within the tiny town limits. A rush outside to the front porch revealed no fountains of burning debris, flame-trailing burst propane tanks or black billowing smoke plumes marring the cloudless blue sky.

Heck, what did I know? I was still a fresh oblivious greenhorn in this weird and wonderful ghost town. Maybe hopeful solo miners were still blasting out test pits. Something to do with what was left of the Drumlummon Mine? Originally from Kansas, I've long ago learned that gunfire itself is as common in rural Montana as hot Oakland nights. As far as I knew (or half

Marysville at its 1895 peak. *Marysville Pioneer Society.*

expected), setting off sticks of dynamite was as common in the Treasure State as my own teenage foolishness of heating up aerosol spray cans until they burst in flaming mini-mortars.

I was reassured to see the noise had also brought my neighbor and longtime resident Vanessa Soboyna to her porch. At least this time, backyard dynamite tosses didn't turn out to be my latest Rocky Mountain recreational surprise.

"Wow." It was my first time speaking to Vanessa past waves and casual hellos. "Is there still some mining going on? Stuff like that a normal thing up here?"

Smiling, she shook her head with shared surprise, answering a single, firm *absolutely not* to both questions. A later walk around town showed nothing out of the ordinary. At least as far as my limited experience allowed.

Oh, well.

LIFE GOT TOO BUSY to dwell on that single distraction. I knew too few of my neighbors at the time and never found out the cause of that strange series of explosive sounds. Idle musings must include consideration of a few critical issues of local topography. Originally a swampy, roughly mile-square bowl that was assiduously avoided by early miners en route to the higher digs, Marysville sits surrounded on three sides by mountain ridges. There are nearly one thousand feet of steep sloping walls to (roughly) the north and south, while to the west rises forested mountain all the way to the Continental Divide. Without the thick bands of Douglas fir and gully-choked cottonwoods, residents could face out the eastern sky down Silver Creek Canyon. Any loud sound in or near town is echoed and amplified by the natural amphitheater. All around are state, federal and other public lands, in addition to large private ranches that allow hunting access.

Gunfire has *not* been unusual. Even out of hunting seasons. Even hearing it, occasionally at least, close enough to guess it originates if not inside technical "city limits" themselves then certainly within a quarter mile of occupied residences. It is not a daily occurrence to be sure, but every once in a while. Enough to take a look (especially in this crazy age), although not necessarily enough for alarm. That big random explosion did not recur, but the strange phantom shots were another thing.

Those double *bangs* continued, on and off, at unrecorded intervals for over a year.

THE BUNKHOUSE SITS HIGH on Grand Street, the backyard clear and empty to the last northern stretch of Main Street. Another empty boulder-and weed-choked field lies across the street, abandoned but for a few ancient test pits and the usual random rockpile lines of old foundations. The slope rises steeply after the first thirty yards, disappearing into the thick tree line.

The field continues downhill, interrupted only by Aspen Way, a small spur cul-de-sac cutting directly west off Main Street to accommodate three homes, an abandoned ruin and the ancient Marysville Post Office at the base of a sharp rise of slope and trees. In my two years at the Bunkhouse, there were multiple times when I heard gunshots (always in pairs although not specifically noted at the time) that seemed to originate in that big field. But there never seemed to be any visible cause. The field was always empty, devoid of hunters or humans.

The natural echo effect, of course. Gunfire in the woods outside town was being reflected back by the western slopes, making it sound like it was coming from the empty field across Main Street. I assumed this was also the explanation for the faint but utterly distinct childish cries that were heard on multiple occasions from around the same area. A little boy calling out for a dog or sibling? The first couple times I trotted down for a peek, half expecting to see some lost kid wandering around, only to greet empty breezes. And no children resided on Aspen Way.

This was a little more disconcerting than misplaced gunshots until, with warming weather, I finally clued in to the large family living at the top of Third Street, directly east across the bowl in which the town sat and in perfect stadium seating line-of-sight to the empty field. With several young kids racing around the yard, every shout, cry or laugh would project without obstruction. The sounds of their active play became a commonplace backdrop to warm weather.

Just…odd that nothing ever seemed to echo back besides faint cries and gunshots.

MONTHS LATER, WHEN TALKING to a neighbor soon after Halloween, I commented on the many great local decorations but thought the recent spate of close gunfire might be a little dangerous for any trick-or-treaters.

Instead of a hearty agreement, I got that particular knowing Marysville gleam in the eye that told me I was missing something. A new lesson for the greenhorn.

"You mean those double shots across in that field?"

Town view in the late 1800s. *Marysville Pioneer Society.*

An unidentified group of Marysville residents on a climbing trip. *Marysville Pioneer Society.*

The specificity was startling. Although I couldn't testify they always came in pairs, it did seem to match my impression, and I nodded. "Yeah. Those in particular."

"No need to worry. Those shots have already done their killing."

By an infamous Marysville woman who, 120 years ago, partly succeeded in an insane attempt to murder her entire family.

Whether she was fueled by evil, mental illness or both, newspapers of the time revealed that an attempted mass killing was indeed true. Included in the accounts was chilling evidence that a thirst for homicide simmered in the woman long before her appearance in Marysville. And that she may already have gotten away with a terrible infanticide. Although taking fictional liberty to mortar together core facts, this is my impression of the murderess drawn from newspaper accounts.

MID-1890s

HELENA, MONTANA

The first time Edith May Wilmot Allen tried to kill her husband, she used a hatchet.

Strong as the impulse was, Mrs. John Wright Allen's tactics were sloppy, and John survived the attack with only an ugly hairline gash where his thick skull deflected the blunt blade—and a frightening new respect for his wife's so-called nervous spells.

Perhaps, Edith mused later, the past dozen years of a passionless but admittedly comfortable marriage had delivered an unconscious last-second hesitation or merciful twinge that turned the intended direct, full-swing strike into a glancing blow. This notion was soon rejected when she was finally getting honest with herself. It wasn't a rustle of regret but the very real and very audible rustle of her long skirt that billowed out from the fierce rush of ambush attack, brushing against the woodstove tongs and rattling just enough to catch John's ear.

John's unexpected turn saved his life.

Edith had meant to cleave the back of his skull.

The Allens were living in their 819 Broadway Street home in Helena, and the ruckus soon attracted neighbors and municipal authorities. The explanation that Edith had mistaken her husband for a burglar was accepted by the scowling police about as much as the excuse of a random meteorite strike. But this was the late 1890s, well on its way to the Great Enlightenment of the twentieth century yet still a time when minor observations such as claims of an intruder in broad daylight at the exact time of Mr. Allen's routine arrival home were shrugged off or ignored. As the *Helena Independent* would later report, "The story was not given credence by the police at the time, but it was no one's business but their [the Allens'] own." A man's home was his castle, his wife and family ultimately serfs, and despite a few anxious glances at the little lady, the king was proffering no charges, accusations or conflicting claims.

Hatchet-wielding wives were not a police concern.

EDITH WAS PLEASED TO discover that getting away with attempted murder was—presently, at least—as calming and satisfactory as getting away with the real thing. This was unexpected. Would assassin snipers be happy with merely winging their target? The charging savannah cat's appetite slated by a swiped claw and a few snatched hairs?

Of course not.

However, in her case at least, it turned out that the attempt in itself was enough to quiet the sociopath within. At least for a while. Perhaps the evil would have slept hidden for years had her first kill been a grown adult like John and not simply their newborn infant. It even made a sort of sense if you thought of it in terms of mathematics. After all, Darby was barely three weeks old when Edith flung him from his crib against the hard wood-and-plaster-lathe walls of the nursery. Mathematically speaking, killing one helpless infant hardly equaled an adult. An imbalance of basic equations.

That had been ten months earlier, and while there was plenty of suspicion, nobody had done a thing. With the recall came her twisted sense of pride.

A single terminal line drive was enough to do the job, but just in case, Edith had used Darby's swaddling blanket and several twisting yanks to ensure a broken neck.

Then Edith had noticed certain telltale divots in the wall plaster. After finding hammer and nail, a simple rehanging of Giovanni Alderchi's *Summer Sparrows in Flight* took care of that business just fine. The bright print of soaring birds across a cloud-choked European sky hung a bit low to her decorator tastes, but adjusting down the still life (here she unconsciously chuckled at the term) by a few inches eliminated the Alderchi piece from standing out. Nobody noticed. Nobody *ever* noticed.

Cheerfully whistling a random tune, Edith had then used the narrow end of the hammer to first pry loose and then break one side of the crib's gate latches, letting it fall open, askew in its tracks but with plenty of room for a baby to tumble out.

Gathering up the loose-limbed, silent and bleeding form at her feet, Edith carefully positioned Darby at the edge of the mattress—now a four-foot cliff edge to the wooden floor—and dropped the lifeless burden to unceremoniously *fluump* down in a sickening half-bounce. Edith considered the scene. Did it sufficiently represent the suggested tragic accident?

Almost.

The swaddling blanket wrapped Darby like a mummy. Too much cushioning. Edith picked him up once more, paying close attention to shake out an already-bruising head on its short stalk of loose boneless neck before a second, more "credible" drop.

John wasn't due home for nearly an hour. After replacing the hammer in its kitchen drawer, there was plenty of time to practice her anguished shrieks. It had been difficult not to laugh in glee instead. Two other small children were enough burden. They were soon to move up to the bustling mining town of Marysville, and the last thing Edith wanted to drag along was a squalling baby.

BLOODY DAWN

John Wright Allen and Edith May Wilmot were married in 1884. Mr. Allen worked in Helena as an assistant melter with the U.S. Assay Office for about ten years. For twelve years before she was married, Edith worked as a domestic maid for U.S. postmaster John C. Curtin. Mr. Allen was described by the *Helena Independent* as a capable man before "becoming a physical wreck" from an addiction to cigarettes. As for his new wife, "There had been rumors of the results of her temper before, but they had been carefully guarded and few knew the truth." The couple had three children: Dorothy, Wilmot and, at least for a short time, little Darby.

After losing his position under unspecified circumstances, Mr. Allen found another job as a watchman for the Belmont Mine—and later the Drumlummon—and so the family moved up to Marysville. They resided there for almost two full years before Edith's madness nearly brought the whole family to a bloody and violent end.

Following is the initial story carried by newspapers of what exactly happened that horrendous October morning.

About forty minutes after the family's 5:00 a.m. wake-up routine, Edith was busy making breakfast for her family when she heard her husband scolding their eleven-year-old boy, Wilmot, for some unspecified transgression. Wilmot's reply was rude, disrespectful or otherwise lame enough to anger his father, who then snatched up the young boy and gave him the whip.

The sight of Wilmot's violent and unjust—to Edith—punishment thrust her into a rage of temporary insanity. She immediately grabbed a .32-caliber rifle leaning against a nearby wall and opened fire on John. The first wild shot winged a chair. The second bullet tragically struck little Wilmot on his left side, immediately dropping the boy to a tangled heap on the floor. The third shot hit its intended target with devastating effect, blasting through John's left humerus and deflecting into his forehead.

Confronting her terrible mistake did nothing to break Edith's fury. She briefly struggled to reload, ensuring fresh lead to finish off her husband.

But despite the bleeding and grave wounds, John had managed to pick himself up and rush out the back door, shrieking for help to a growing crowd of alarmed neighbors. He then stumbled inside, smashing into his infuriated wife and yanking the smoking rifle away. A man identified as Mr. Schlater had heard the blasts and screams and raced to the scene in time to assist John in restraining Edith. Still hotly enraged, Edith fought long and hard against both men, forcing Schlater to throw her to the floor and hold her down until the constable arrived—on the heels of half the town, attracted by the raucous early morning commotion.

Wilmot lived for only a few scarce minutes after Mr. Schlater's arrival. The man reported hearing the boy's last mournful words with his own ears: "Momma shot me. I'll never forgive her."

Upon arrival of the law, Edith became "remarkably calm for a woman who had just killed her child and almost made a widow of herself." This and other quotes here are from the *Helena Independent* of October 30, 1896.

Doctors were called to attend the yet-alive, greatly suffering John. Edith was escorted over to Mr. Schlater's home while authorities tried to sort things out. Notifications went out to County Attorney R.R. Purcell and Thomas Pleasants, coroner. Via train and wagon, both arrived in Marysville by the afternoon to conduct an immediate juried inquest. It did not take the jury long to conclude Wilmot Allen died via gunfire from his mother, Edith, gripped at the time by a fit of temporary insanity. On that verdict and further obvious advice, it was ordered that Mrs. Allen be brought down to Helena for judicial examination and closer looks at the state of her mental condition.

She would make this trip under armed guard after a few clarifying details the jury was able to hear, painfully whispered over the bloodstained bed of her shot-up husband.

"Recollections of School Year 1895–96." Precise identifications of many individuals do not survive. However, this group shot may be critical as the only extant image of eleven-year-old Wilmot Allen—buried in anonymity with the rest of the unidentified children—presumably the school year preceding his October 1896 murder. *Marysville Pioneer Society.*

JOHN REPORTED NO ARGUMENT between father and son—no transgressions, no shouts or snippy talk-backs and certainly no violent whippings. John struggled out his testimony between gritted teeth of pain as Dr. Landstrom and assistants tended his dreadful wounds. There had been nothing much at all because John hadn't yet gotten out of bed before he felt a confused shock of suddenly waking from a loud blast and abrupt, overwhelming pain in his arm and head. John berated himself for not acting quicker. Who could blame him? Justifiably stunned, John tottered out of bed, dimly aware of his wife in the kitchen, leaning over and busy with some long object.

A rifle.

Trembling with so much rage she was fumbling with the reload.

It was about this moment when Wilmot appeared on the scene, rushing out from his bedroom and attempting to "pacify" his crazed mother by hugging her tight and "whispering words of love," only to get angrily shoved away, "reeling backwards."

Above: Body cooler #1. The lonely approach to the ornate stone vault for expired miners and district residents who perished during the winter months and awaited ground thaw. It was originally planned as the centerpiece for the vast, 1,700-plot Mountain View Cemetery, which was never completed. The few burials before abandonment were long moved to other established cemeteries. *Author photo.*

Opposite, top: Body cooler #2. The armored outer door. The author presumes this prevented wandering grizzlies from stealing any "frozen burritos," as well as containing any pesky outbreaks of vampires and/or zombies. *Author photo.*

Opposite, bottom: Body cooler #3. The double set of doors is open. *Author photo.*

Into a perfect target position.

Edith swept up the gun and fired, blasting Wilmot at point-blank range.

Now poised over her bleeding son, Edith scrambled with another furious reload. This is what John testified he saw through the blood pouring into his eyes, having pulled himself into the room and, despite his injuries, wrestled the gun away from a wife who "fought like a giantess," opened a door and threw the rifle out. Schlater showed up as initially reported, taking over the brunt of the battle from an exhausted, collapsing John.

The many others who quickly arrived added their testimony. They had seen how Wilmot managed to reach his bed after a couple stumbling attempts, lamely covering himself up as he bled heavily from a chest wound. Shocked neighbors could do little but witness his last words were indeed a mournful indictment: "My mother shot me. I'll never forgive her for it."

The inquest jury also heard from Dorothy, the eight-year-old daughter of John and Edith, who had been standing near. Her most important contribution was reporting she had never before seen her father strike Wilmot except for one time when John used a thin stick to whack a naughty Wilmot. She never saw her father hit Edith, and as far as she was concerned, "she was sure her father and mother lived pleasantly and peacefully together."

Dorothy was presumed to be target number three, saved only because of her father's desperate intervention as killer mom struggled to reload the murder weapon.

THE STRANGE CALM THAT overtook Edith did not last by the time she arrived the next day at the hospital in Helena. "She was much excited and appeared to the attendants to be on the verge of complete collapse." After a doctor finally got her settled down (assuredly with the help of sedatives), Edith was deemed unable to be cared for there and was shipped off to the "county hospital" early that afternoon. "William Stuewe, superintendent of the poor farm, last night said that she appeared to be improved but that her condition was still critical....The question of Mrs. Allen's sanity will not be inquired into until her physical condition improved."

Two months later, the *Mountaineer* reported that Edith Allen would plead not guilty to a charge of first-degree murder. Little Wilmot was laid to rest in the Marysville Cemetery just northeast of town. His marker and exact plot location are lost. John Allen apparently survived. He and his daughter Dorothy both vanished into history, hopefully going on to rebuild their lives and sanity, far from the lurid newspaper accounts.

ANALYSIS AND DISCUSSION

2017

My Marysville neighbor let the newcomer connect the dots on his own.

I understand the implication: those seemingly sourceless, randomly occurring pair of shots to be the phantom echoes of a crazed Edith Allen trying to wipe out her family. That event had happened two days before Halloween, thus the perception that, although the shots could be heard throughout the year, they're more likely to be heard around trick-or-treat time. The faint children's cries? Why, the spirit of Wilmot of course, yet berating his mother with his dying words.

Chilling story. And absolutely true. At least the Allen one.

But are these shots and faint cries heard today the ghostly echoes of that tragic day? Not so sure. That first random explosion hasn't fit in with any account.

A key confirming detail has been lost over the intervening 120 years. Or, to be fair, not yet found. Namely the specific address of the Allen home in October 1896. Had it actually been in those abandoned fields to either side of today's Aspen Way? If so, it would add greatly to the stories as well as the possibility of the audio anomalies turning out to be true GSE phenomena. It has also been pointed out that with the natural amphitheater effect, the Allen home only had to be fairly close to rate. At the very least, the situation demands some closer scrutiny—and multiple recording devices—especially around late October.

By all modern interpretations, Edith Allen suffered from serious mental illness. But when are sympathetic kid gloves traded for an iron hand and cuffs? Definitely when a person becomes an active threat intent on homicide. Despite the fictionalization of Darby's suspected death, is it unfair to depict Edith as a cunning, would-be serial killer? There was surely no tactical subtlety in suddenly deciding to blast away the entire fam-damly early one morning. How was she planning to explain away *that* one? A whole bunch of intruders this time and no nearby hatchet to fend 'em off?

Extreme postpartum depression or other debilitating conditions could explain Darby and everything else. That event might have been a true accident. Those "rumors of the results of her temper" may have nothing to do with it. Same with the mood swings: "at times sullen and excitable…times when she was dangerous to approach." Yet had modern mental healthcare been available, it's likely Edith would have been a different, better person living out a happy life with loving family.

Body cooler #4. The grim interior. *Author photo.*

Body cooler #5. An interior view with top vent. *Author photo.*

Body cooler #6. An exterior view to the side with the outlet vent pipe. *Author photo.*

Impossible to know, of course. Most killers are presumed insane at a basic level, aren't they? Suspicions about Darby's death suggest Edith may have been covering something up. Murder or terrible accident, circumstances also suggest premeditated action.

No matter the root cause or causes, we can be grateful that wholesale slaughter was prevented by a heroic father who refused to lie down and bleed.

CHAPTER 4

UNSETTLED SPIRITS
AT MARYSVILLE HOUSE

Late at night, if it's real quiet…you might still hear that old ghost train whistle.
—Marysville House menu

"WORTH THE RIDE"

For those who believe in reincarnation, look no further than Marysville House Historic Bar & Steakhouse. This unique structure rates a special status as a rare survivor of the (then raucous and rambunctious) late 1880s town of Silver City, six miles down-canyon. Over a century after that busy mining town/railroad hub's heyday, just about every physical sign has vanished. No old sagging outbuildings or cabins. No signs or historical markers. Not even any piles of sun-bleached lumber. Silver City has been reduced to an obscure set of GPS coordinates of lonely, empty prairie.

All except for Marysville House (MvH), first built as the bustling Northern Pacific Railroad station for Silver City and still standing proud and strong today, thriving in its new role as the premier restaurant, bar and gathering place this side of the Continental Divide. Although I am incredibly partial to the menu myself and a blatant fan, the five-star quality of food, service and atmosphere is backed up by reputation and the vast majority of published reviews. The kitchen stars a master St. Louis chef backed by a staff of friendly locals who care deeply about making your experience a memorable one. After all, it's not just their job. It's their *home*.

Modern Marysville House. *Author photo.*

Credibility of quality has been established for years. It is of no unfair advantage that, noting an obvious relevant fact, Marysville House is not just the best but the *only* restaurant, bar and gathering place this side of the Continental Divide—at least in the local neighborhood. The Silver City Saloon operates some seven miles distant and a few thousand feet down and out of the canyon. And there's probably fifteen times the traffic daily going through the Great Divide Ski Area's snack bar than MvH's best day—but then again, only during the ski season.

There's no doubt Marysville House Historic Bar & Steakhouse is definitely Worth the Ride.

MvH's Original Role

When serving as the busy Northern Pacific Railroad station down in Silver City, the building was a routine stopping point from Montana Territory's burgeoning future capital city of Helena to Great Falls to the great riverboat landings of Fort Benton—a local version of Grand Central Station.

Today's portion of the Maryville House bar was yesterday's railroad stationmaster office and passenger lobby. Windows were strategically placed

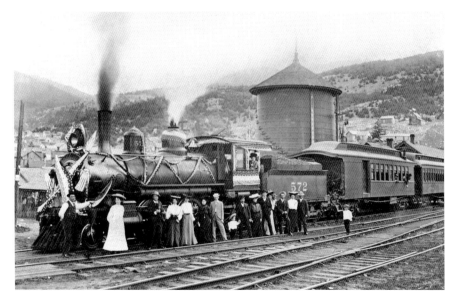

Old 572 locomotive at Marysville station. *Marysville Pioneer Society.*

for spotting approaching trains from either east or west. The thick log walls of the dining room once held thousands of tons of baggage and freight for the pioneers carving out their frontier destinies. The building is most definitely a living "relic" from the Old West.

But as far as its Marysville location is considered, this particular structure is a relatively fresh neighbor. It was "only" about four decades ago in 1975 that Rick O'Connell of the same-name pioneer family rescued the station from the fast-disappearing bones of Silver City for permanent relocation to its current 153 Main Street site in Marysville. It was moved here to renew a tradition dating back to at least the 1890s: look close at the many military appreciation plaques and vintage photos on the wall and you may see the *original* Marysville House. This was a café and boardinghouse beside the opera house on Grand.

OLDEST HONORS

As I don't consider the long-existing Freemasons a "business," it should nonetheless be noted that the local Ottawa Lodge in Marysville (established in town long before the still-standing, still-used Mason Hall was built in 1898 after the first meeting in a Continental Divide field) has held meetings contiguously since then. In my analysis, it rates honors for the longest continuously operating organization of any kind in the area, business or otherwise.

When it comes to the oldest business *structure* in Marysville that still has an operating business, the ribbon goes to the connected pair of long stone buildings across the street and a bit south—first built in 1886 as the Dillon Livery but more popularly known after its 1900s conversion into the Cotton Club Dance Hall and Saloon. Boasting a breathtaking restoration, the location is now open as a unique setting for parties, weddings and celebratory events of all kinds.

Today's Marysville "business district" couldn't compete with the tiniest mini-mall, but it's enough for at least a steady heartbeat of commerce. Along with the lingering residents, it's more than enough to stave off most of the dead "ghost town" accusations. Most would think—if there really were spirits watching in the ethereal background—that this stubborn streak of commercial vitality would be cause for pride. This might be so at the "new" Marysville Historic General Store and Cotton Club Dance Hall: no worker, owner or staff has admitted to the slightest hint of GSE activity, and personally witnessing several of their parties spilling into the streets showed nothing but happy people and good times.

Marysville House Historic Bar & Steakhouse has some different stories.

It's only in the last few generations that speaking about being a witness to ghosts and other supernatural events wouldn't instantly get you labeled as a fanciful nutcase with negative consequences to everything from employment to personal reputation. Some of that judgmental dismissal still exists, but even most self-declared skeptics agree that *something unusual* must be at work. The subject is no longer instantly denigrated and rates today as one of our most popular cultural interests.

Similarly, having a business known or suspected to be "haunted" is no longer a bad thing. As a matter of fact, the U.S. Commerce Department has recognized a substantial profit advantage to those businesses that gain such a reputation. It's gotten to the point that some people have faked GSEs in desperate schemes to gain the claim of being haunted. The activity at Marysville House has a solid, confident reputation without hype. It simmers in the background, unknown to most, without affecting business in the least.

A STRATEGIC SUICIDE

Once upon a time...

The (conveniently unnamed) Silver City stationmaster felt he had given his life to the (it is assumed) Northern Pacific Railroad. His late 1870s assignment to the mining camp hub out on the prairie was a hard-earned reward for years of service. His loyalty was such that he rarely left the station, bunking in his office and gaining a reputation as the hardest-working stationmaster on the entire line. Sometime around the early 1890s silver panic, facing the realities of Silver City's decline and an unconscionable retirement, the despairing man threw himself in front of a speeding locomotive.

Thus, Mr. Unnamed Master becomes a ghost to forever haunt his beloved station.

Depending on the opinion, the phantom's ire is: just garden-variety "mean spirit" stuff; jealousy at the good times, high-life meals, drinks and atmosphere taking place around it; or anger at the station's relocation and/or its change from a transportation workhorse to a celebratory place of food, drink and relaxation.

A Marysville-bound train boards at Helena station, armed for mountain snow. *Marysville Pioneer Society.*

Tourists on the Northern Pacific Railroad trestle into town with the slope of Drumlummon Mine in the background. It is a cheerful enough group, but futile speculations overwhelm all guesses as to any purpose or occasion depicted. *Marysville Pioneer Society.*

LEVITATING BOTTLES

Rumor turns to unequivocal fact when the most wondrous Marysville House GSE events are witnessed.

Bartender Chris Boyles reports this incident occurring not long ago—a few years—indicating that spiritual energies are still active. He tells of standing at the end of the bar nearest the door, talking to Roger, a local resident living down-canyon on the old Silver City site. Roger was sitting at the mid-point of the bar, facing the double shelves of liquor bottles.

"We're talking….He's having dinner, having a drink. And the bottles came up…levitated over the top of the other bottles [in the front row], over to the mat then dropped."

A succinct and calm (if a bit wide-eyed) summary of an anti-gravity poltergeist. Two bottles were involved, both mostly full and quite heavy, neither breaking when falling on the rubber floor mat. Nothing else happened while the shocked guys asked the normal *Did you see THAT?* and ensured there had been no hallucination.

IDENTIFIED FLYING OBJECTS

Rogue nation missile tests were never much of an issue for Marysville House customers "many years ago" because they had concerns of their own much closer to home, such as the seemingly unprovoked, surprise ballistic launches of objects off tables in both bar and dining room.

Obviously, no nukes were involved, yet the sudden surprise flights of table candles and/or flowerpot centerpieces could be as unsettling as North Korean rockets. Sometimes more so—no injuries had ever been reported, but the trajectories of these small but solid flying objects have shared the upsetting commonality of picking people as their targets. Unlike the random occurrences of the usual poltergeist, an unsuspecting person always seemed to be sitting or standing at the end of these trajectories.

Fortunately, the vast majority of incidents resulted in near-misses or close calls. And while the table candles were light votives in small glass holders, the throws were violent with clear hostile intent—those standing might have one bounce off a hip or thigh without suffering a bruise, but those sitting down risked a head strike and potentially serious injury. Despite the powerful force launching these objects across rooms, its ultimate aim was more erratic or, as some suggest, more interested in fright than injury. A "shot across the bow" warning versus blatant attack.

The backbone of this reported activity involves an unnamed woman customer who in the dim unspecific past had witnessed several of these flying object incidents, with several near-misses of her own. The deal-breaker came with a short-range launch off the same table at which she was sitting, enjoying a meal with friends. Without warning and "so the story goes," the candleholder leapt off the table directly in front of this woman, shattering her wineglass and then thumping into her shoulder with the force of a center-drive pitch.

She was splashed and startled but unhurt, according to the accounts. There was mention of her wearing a winter coat or other heavy garment, with the point being that her fright was more at the *potential* of injury than any actual sustained physical damage. Her pledge never to return was reluctant, as she absolutely loved the food, company and atmosphere. Some epilogues say this out-of-town lady is still a loyal customer—but only on a takeout basis, refusing to enter past a few steps. A few say she's got a free-meals-for-life comp deal because of the disturbing events.

Free Marysville House meals for life? *Batter up, phantoms!*

ANALYSIS AND DISCUSSION

Three years after hearing these welcome-to-the-neighborhood town stories and official GSE investigation began, what does eager follow-up reveal on the tables at the Marysville House Historic Bar & Steakhouse of today?

Little glass candleholders and/or small flowerpot centerpieces.

If dangerous flying objects were *that* much of a concern, this was the GSE equivalent of setting up an active minefield in your own front yard. Official word is that the surprise centerpiece artillery was a big problem "many years ago" and not a modern concern. Most people would translate that as not an issue whatsoever. The reports of the flying candleholders—at least the core details—are adamantly defended as truth. What about the rest?

TRAIN-JUMPER OR CLAIM-JUMPER?

The suicidal stationmaster source is "known" if, thanks to me, equally useless for clarification or confirmation. That's because it came from a friendly, sixty-something couple who drove up my first summer and asked for directions to the cemetery.

My excuse would be my yet-unappreciated awareness of the town's stunning history, but I still cringe at not asking for a reference name or trusting recall for which out-of-state license plate their vehicle bore. Today, Florida feels as appropriate as Ohio. Used to live here themselves or have close family here? That too sounds right, yet how could past residents forget where the cemetery's been for the last 150 years?

I vividly recall the short roadside conversation, the first time I learned Marysville House was originally built as a railroad station in Silver City

Beloved "Old 572" locomotive on Marysville trestle, 1915. *Marysville Pioneer Society.*

and was supposed to be haunted by that stationmaster. I don't recall what manifestations that was supposed to entail (probably, as is my style, I interrupted and eventually scared off the guy with my own babble).

What about the woman customer struck by a candleholder and rewarded with a lifetime comp? The current operators report nothing like that in their memory, no secret VIPs, and Chef Brian Hammerschmidt denies any free-meals-for-life programs—and began reaching for a carving knife when I suggested it when falsely claiming I got beaned myself.

Routine checks of the freely available newspaper sources hold no story about well-known (or any, for that matter) railroad stationmasters throwing themselves in front of trains. Generally speaking, this means it's probably nothing more than a tall tale or transplanted archetype because it would have been such a sensational story that it would have been covered by the lurid newspapers of the time, particularly in Marysville and Helena. Silver City wasn't that isolated and had once been considered the logical choice of state capital.

Nevertheless, it cannot be claimed that each and every newspaper was checked for each day of the last ten years of the nineteenth century. For now, it looks pretty unlikely, but the case of the suicidal stationmaster—and whether the story is connected whatsoever with Marysville House—remains on the active list for further collaboration and/or documentation.

SCHNAPPS OR SNAKE OIL?

Credible witness reports establish the flying bottles as truth. "I know Chris Boyles. Chris Boyles is my friend." Personally looking into his eyes versus evaluating street rumor banished any doubt for me that he and Roger witnessed two heavy liquor bottles rise up out of their place and intelligently maneuver over their front-row obstructions to horizontally sail at least two feet against gravity. Note period at end of last sentence.

Typical interior of one of Marysville's approximately twenty-seven saloons operating in boom years. *Marysville Pioneer Society.*

CHAPTER 5

TRICKY TELEPORTATIONS AND SPECTERS OF THE STREETS

There have been many investigated cases of the miraculous transportation of persons or things over great distances in an instant. It's called "teleportation." It has something to do with the still-unsolved laws of time and space.
—*John Newland, host of* One Step Beyond, *1959*

TRICKY TELEPORTATIONS

Dave Larson (not his real last name) looked puzzled, followed by that familiar reluctant sigh of a person deciding to relate an inexplicable personal event without a shred of expectation he'd be believed. Dave didn't so much tell his story as he did confess it. That's because, like the poltergeist attack to the cowboy in the Red House, it was so strange he just couldn't fit it into the world he knew. He was fully aware of "how it sounded" and couldn't blame anybody for thinking he'd dreamt the whole thing.

Except Dave was wide awake when it occurred.

And he was also dead certain that "whatever it was" did more than scare the hell out of him. It also saved his life.

No doubts of credibility whatsoever. I went to high school with Dave. I knew him to be a down-to-earth guy, not one prone to wild fantasies or the crazier antics of youth. Athlete swimmer. High academics. Math whiz. No smoking, drinking or drugs. Hard worker with after-school jobs, along with a firm plan for college and building his future. Dave had so

Betsy with ruins. *Author photo.*

much of his stuff together I was frequently amazed he associated with me and my near-delinquent, geeky crowd. Dave simply didn't shove people into the typical high school castes and chose to associate with whomever he wanted.

It was about five years after graduation when I visited the old south Kansas City neighborhood and ran into my old friend. Dave looked hale and hearty, focused life as much on track as mine was off the rails. Exactly how we ever got onto such a weird subject is lost to the mists of time. Bizarre things had already been occurring in my life, and perhaps we were comparing notes. I do remember Dave's second thoughts at first mention, trying to wave it aside or dismiss—only relating the account after plenty of picking and prodding, as well as a firm pledge not to call up, as Dave put it, "the boys with the white coats and the big butterfly nets."

No worries there, I promised. "I've been ducking those guys for years. Tell me what happened."

COLLISION COURSE

A large office building in an even larger midwestern office park.

Dave was working some kind of entry-level desk job for a forgotten company that shared the huge, blocky six-story building with multiple other businesses. Below ground level, there was a network of large connecting tunnels that serviced everything from adjoining warehouses to large cafeterias, stores and restaurants. As such, these broad, well-lighted tunnels carried about as much activity as the streets above—mostly foot traffic by the business employees and their vendors—but also had a "motorized only" lane along one wall reserved for electric carts and forklifts.

Nothing separated the foot traffic from the mechanical besides yellowjacket warning stripes on the floor.

"Completely distracted." Dave taps his temple. "Something about work…important at the time, I guess, but who knows now, right?" Dave was completely preoccupied as he trotted down the access stairs for the underground hallway en route to a nearby cafeteria. He didn't process the signs or recognize the danger, deep in thought as he bounced off the last step. He pulled open a door and, without hesitation, strode into the tunnel with a sharp righthand turn toward the cafeteria…

…directly into the path of a fast-rolling forklift.

"A 'speeding forklift' sounds goofy, but man, let me tell you it was faster than walking speed and no time to dodge. Not carrying anything. Its metal lift tongs were at about the level of my chest." Dave insists it was all his fault—his distracted brain, his sudden appearance out of a stairwell and his own quick trot right into the thing. Dave does not have to outstretch his arms far to illustrate the gap between him and certain death. A flashing glimpse of shock on the forklift operator's face, maybe a fractional second or two was left to Dave to wonder if he'd be first speared, possibly decapitated by one of the steel lift tongs or merely crushed on sheer impact.

"*Blink!*" Dave snaps his fingers.

"Next moment, I'm standing a few feet farther down the corridor—*behind* the forklift that was cramming on its brakes, tilting forward, screeching side to side as the guy stood on the pedal. It almost fell over. A bunch of people noticed, began pointing and shouting, but nobody noticed me because they were all looking at the skidding forklift. They all thought he locked up his brakes, ran something over that should have been *me*, but there was nothing there. I somehow blinked over to the other side."

Some would call that instantaneous teleportation.

Dave doesn't know *what* process or force was at work, only that it absolutely prevented him from being squashed, impaled or both. His practical nature insists on the reality as equally as it presents questions so inexplicable he simply cannot come to any conclusion besides deep gratitude. Guardian angel, spontaneous time displacement or some fantastic innate, unconscious natural ability—there was no way to know. Dave believes that despite the "good ending," the incident will haunt him for the rest of his life.

Perhaps some humans—under extremely particular conditions—can unconsciously trigger a natural ability to emergency transport. If so, the percentage is as infinitesimal as the reports are rare. However, once identified through such an experience, those individuals might present the opportunity for more definitive scientific testing than most GSE phenomena—but it's doubtful anybody would agree to experiments that would require sudden no-warning shoves off tall buildings or into the paths of speeding buses.

As defined by Webster, *teleportation* sounds more like the classic *Star Trek* transporter: "The theoretical transportation of matter through space by converting it into energy and then re-converting it at the terminal point." More traditional references don't specify any theoretical processes, considered simply as objects being made to move through space under the influence of mental forces alone. It's usually considered a form of psychokinesis if not the latter's strict definition.

Nineteenth-century British medium Mrs. Samuel Guppy was reported to demonstrate this talent in a peculiar manner. As described in *Encyclopedia of the Unexplained*, she "produced live lobsters and eels, and fresh flowers, fruit and vegetables apparently out of nowhere at her seances." On the surface at least, this may have been nothing more than a unique twist on the many charlatans of the time.

Can this very same phenomena of teleportation—or one like it—be demonstrated among the many reports of Marysville GSEs? According to Steve Soboyna, there's no doubt about it. And although the experiences of him and his wife, Vanessa, thankfully lacked the extreme drama of instant escapes from imminent death—they were more on the level of minor mischief—the oft-recurring events were equally inexplicable.

And weird enough to suspect a GSE.

WINTER 2017

A-ha! Fresh prey out in the open!

As a hungry orca coming up on an unwary seal, my snowbound tromp down to the mailboxes was diverted by the unusual spectacle of my professional excavator neighbor Andy Phillips wrangling a snorting mini-Bobcat (along with loyal beagle assistant Samwise in easy reach of controls), engrossed in his level professional best with the apparent goal of ripping off Steve Soboyna's front porch roof.

This strange structural assault was more curiosity than concern.

The new guy was learning that things didn't always turn out as they first appear in this town. Andy was a nice guy, friends with the Soboynas, and if he needed to bash a modest piece of smokin' construction equipment through their front porch, I'm sure there was a good reason. Consent was obvious—Steve the homeowner himself was bundled up right there in the yard, displaying no sign of distress and heartily shouting helpful suggestions.

He was my primary target, perfectly positioned for a "walk-by" quickie interview, right there on the street without need for making appointments or, for me at the time, uncomfortable knocking on doors to snoop out rumors. Interest in pinning down all the crazy GSE reports was at its height, and here was a golden opportunity to weed out the truth behind one of the milder—if more bizarre—reports.

It was another case of doubt whether I heard things right the first time. Joke on the greenhorn snooper? Yes and no. After multiple sources told me to talk to the Soboynas, the basic rumors turned out to be consistent. It was not a prank. But c'mon, *really?*

Man-made objects of dark histories—like old ships, James Dean's car or recycled parts from horrific plane crashes—have been reported to be affected by otherworldly forces and perhaps even possessed by evil spirits.

So now we add *light bulbs* to the list?

As it turned out, the foundation of the rumors was built on truth, but as should always be suspected when investigating repeated stories, the finer details required some adjustment. The Soboynas weren't plagued by demons. The light bulbs were merely the central element to a somewhat "unusual" circumstance that kept happening in their previous residence. No big deal. Not harmful. Nothing earth-shattering.

But to explain it? Be our guest.

It was another case of Marysville residence musical chairs.

The house in which the Soboynas used to reside is another beautifully renovated older cabin now occupied by their close friends. Nestled in the midst of town, most of the old crowding neighborhood is long gone, with expansive empty lots adding bonus open space to trimmed lawns. And while the specific site is in dispute, some believe the house lies directly on if not in immediate proximity to founder Thomas Cruse's original cabin from the mid-1870s. Reports of tall, nattily dressed, white-bearded guys in top hats? Wonderful thought, but not a one. Surely Mr. Cruse is otherwise occupied in the afterlife.

This activity was more on the lines of harmless—if annoying to the "victims"—practical joking.

"Damn straight we had problems with light bulbs." Steve frowns, laughing at the same time as I posthole through snowdrifts for my unexpected question. "That's plural. We couldn't keep one *in* the thing!"

Before I can inquire on exactly what the "thing" was, the roar of the Bobcat rumbles off, and I'm able to return Andy's hearty "Happy New Year!" This was weeks ago, but nobody seems to mind. I offer a stumbling apology to Sam that I'm not packing my usual town dog biscuits. Sam is not pleased. I decline a ride offer in the bucket that I hope was jest. The cheery atmosphere hardly fit a madman's bucket-loader attack, and indeed, the truth became evident with the Bobcat's renewed growl and huge crash as it dislodged a piano-sized hunk of ice that would have otherwise brought down Steve's entire roof.

Just another public service, courtesy of Andy Phillips and Sam, Marysville's Heavy Metal Heroes.

Mr. Soboyna told his story.

HOUDINI HIJINKS

For Steve and Vanessa Soboyna, frequent visits by family (that included young grandchildren) were a source of delight as well as concern. Keeping things safe is a priority in all households with kids running around: the little tykes need to be protected from any dangerous stuff lying about the grandparents' house. Common sense. That meant childproof latches for medicine cabinets and areas where cleaning products were stored. Any firearms? Well, any of those required secure placement within a large, solid-wood cabinet equipped with thick doors, shielded hinges and a heavy-duty, built-in key lock. That was also a great place to store important papers. Short of blasting caps or a stout maul, there was no breaking into the thing. The only key was on a single ring used by both wife and husband.

Another feature of this cabinet was the electric light built into the top panel. It really helped with the cabinet's deep, dark shelves. However, ever since the Soboynas had moved into this house and set up the cabinet, they found they would have been better off using candles to look into the thing. Flipping the inside switch was as effective as flipping their noses.

The inside light that never failed before remained dark and lifeless.

Function was no problem. When they first set it up and plugged it in, the interior light popped on as instantly bright and gleeful as ever. Trouble was, every time since then that they unlocked the cabinet, they were greeted with only darkness. It never became unplugged, absent-mindedly or accidentally. All the bulbs were new and tested fine in other lamps. But getting the interior light to come on was patently impossible with the bulb now across the room on a high, dusty shelf—the same bulb each swore was installed inside the cabinet the last time it was locked up, during intervals in which Steve had the key in his possession the entire time.

The weird incident began to repeat itself. Again and again, returning to the locked cabinet showed the light bulb to have been somehow transported to the same dusty shelf across the room. The high shelf with a pile of obstructing boxes below made retrieving the thing—or placing it up there in the first place—awkward and difficult. The shelf was out of reach unless using a stepladder or sturdy chair, neither of which was kept in the room.

After a while, the Soboynas simply gave up trying to keep light bulbs in the cabinet, resorting instead to keeping a flashlight nearby. They never had any problems with that device, even, interestingly enough, once or twice when it was placed inside and forgotten. Whatever force stubbornly refused to allow a light bulb in the interior socket apparently had no problem with the tiny bulb of a flashlight.

A bizarre status quo indeed. And on the scale of local hauntings, a mild GSE that can be easily worked around or all-out ignored—although its manifestations hint of unknown physical processes that could revolutionize our current level of science and technology.

SPIRITS OF THE STREET

Barb Smith is the none-too-imaginative alias given to this Marysville resident not necessarily to protect *her* identity but rather to shield her friend "Jane Jones." Barb was willing to tell what she herself witnessed but insistent that Jane—the main percipient in this GSE case—was so upset at the event that she would likely never speak about it again. Attempting to do so would be asking too much and would threaten their longtime friendship and, worse, according to Barb, risk some real psychological pain by forcing Jane to again confront memories both frightening and inexplicable.

"I SEE DEAD PEOPLE"

Jane was described as "a bit of a nervous type." Perhaps with good reason. For as long as she could remember and *definitely* against her wishes, Jane kept running into ghosts and other supernatural events. Disembodied voices. Visions. All the stuff willing psychics would embrace as great gifts, Jane considered unwanted burdens. Not a blessing but an affliction. She didn't want anything to do with the supernatural. The whole subject was disturbing.

Barb had known about this for as long as she had known her friend. As described, Jane's "problem" wasn't as intense as Haley Joel Osment's daily experiences in *The Sixth Sense*, but like that movie, the glimpses of the spirit world would occur at random intervals with startling effect. She had given up trying to explain them to unbelieving family and only very close friends—like Barb—who didn't attempt to judge, insist on alternate explanations or do much else besides serve as comfort and support for her clearly distressed friend.

These disturbing GSE experiences did not intrude into their friendship. Jane's being supernaturally sensitive became a background point—just something you knew about a person but nothing that defined them on a day-to-day basis. Barb certainly had no such thoughts when Jane finally accepted a longtime open invitation to drive up to Marysville for a nice lunch and afternoon of catching up. They hadn't seen each other since Barb moved up to the mountains. Yet Barb would have happily driven down for a meet in town had she the slightest suspicion a simple friendly visit would thrust her friend into a terrifying encounter with the supernatural.

JANE SEEMED ANXIOUS FROM the very first step into Barb's house. That was Barb's first impression, but it was barely enough to note before the sunny afternoon and happy reunion banished all negative thoughts. Time to laugh over good memories, proudly show off the new house and sit down to a hot, home-cooked lunch.

Soon into the meal, Jane's disquiet grew.

There was nothing wrong with the food—but her self-declared hunger seemed to dissolve away after a few bites. According to Barb, "She [Jane] was really distracted by something. Kept glancing out the window next to the dining room table, sometimes staring for a few moments like she was watching things going on. Turned my head a couple times too, but I never saw anything but empty fields and streets."

At the time, Barb interpreted Jane's discomfort as her being anxious to leave. Like people worried about the time are constantly glancing at watches or clocks, others are drawn to windows and the freedom beyond. Barb didn't take it personally, assuming it was some private concern for Jane alone; maybe her well-known indigestion was acting up and she didn't want to embarrass Barb about an otherwise delightful meal.

Whatever the negative issue might have been, Jane offered nothing but polite thanks, proclaiming all was wonderful about Barb's home, lunch and visit but admitting she underestimated the drive time up to Marysville and, well, the afternoon still held a lot of errands. Lots to do and all that. Better get on the road…great lunch…*bye!*

Standing at her front door, Barb couldn't help but notice Jane's quick, fearful glances to each side before deliberately facing forward and hurrying to her car just short of an outright run. Jane resurrected an uneasy smile out her window as she buckled up, a rather weak wave and then immediately drove off.

Barb always considered Jane a good driver. As evidence to that fact, even in such a clear hurry, she kept her speed down in consideration for neighbors, dogs and dust as she headed down the dirt road. Yet before reaching Marysville Road to disappear down-canyon, Barb was alarmed to see Jane swerve two or three times for no visible reason. Barb had an uphill vantage and could see the entire street. There was nothing for Jane's car to avoid.

Except for phantom pioneer street traffic only she could see.

"WE WERE NOT ALONE"

Although their friendship perseveres, Barb and Jane do not often see each other. Logistics are the reasons—each has a family and busy life, and no longer are they next-door neighbors as in the past. Jane remains in the Capital City, while Barb lives "way up" in Marysville. Schedules conflict and miles separate.

And Jane has no intention of again stepping foot in that high Rockies ghost town.

Why?

It took over a year until Jane admitted her true reason. She wished never to return because in Marysville the ghosts are everywhere—still boldly walking the streets in broad daylight.

A SPECTACLE OF SPIRITS

This was no vague sighting of mist or shadow. What Jane described was looking straight into the past in all its bustling glory. Fully formed people of "throbbing solidity" crowded the sidewalks while wagons, mules, horses and other livestock tromped through streets in billows of dust. These figures were reported to move and appear lifelike except for their generally grainy appearance and only "streaks of color" to their otherwise totally gray tones. Jane could not see through them, but as quoted above, she reported their existence as varying in intensity, details randomly clarifying or blurring out.

All of the traffic were men. Most had long mustaches and beards; several wore more formal jackets, while others, obviously miners and other laborers, strode by with working clothes like overalls, suspenders and muddy boots. A couple carried long-handled picks. One "nattily dressed" individual in a long-tailed coat proudly wore a high hat resembling a stovepipe design, while the others sported a range of hats described as "like bowlers" to soft beret-type caps and "hats like cowboy size but had round brims and looked like felt." This all pretty much matches old photos from the late 1800s and early 1900s.

Jane noted these startling details through the many reluctant glances out the window that Barb, although wildly off-base at the precise cause, took as a growing distraction. And the phantom parade didn't just fade away. Unlike other past visions, this one was impossible to ignore. Worse, the time slip or pioneer replay seemed to be growing in intensity. Figures pulsed, becoming more solid to block out background objects. Jane began to hear the clattering creak of wagons…snorting mules…faint echoes of teamster shouts…thin screel of train whistle…

The breaking point came when Barb went to get them some hot coffee. But half a minute proved to be about twenty seconds too long to leave her friend alone. Reluctant or not, Jane couldn't help but turn back to the window.

The pioneers were still there, in even greater numbers than before: horses, wagons, mules and human foot traffic "overlapping in places. Like a montage but one that was melting." Then her attention was drawn to the most frightening sight of all: another workman or miner with bushy black beard and hair, distinctive from the rest only because this man, of all those around him, was the only thing standing still.

Looking straight at Jane with an expression of wonder.

The man raised an arm, as if shading his eyes with his palm, as he began moving again.

Straight across the short field to Jane's window.

This figure was halfway to the house before Jane fled to her car.

CHAPTER 6

THE ANGRY HUNCHBACK HAG OF DEADMAN CREEK

There is still a calling for the prospector, and that he will still make many discoveries, some of which may prove as valuable as the Granite Mountain, the Anaconda or the Drum Lummon.
—Montana inspector of mines G.C. Swallow, 1896

There were a lot of people running around the Montana Rockies toward the end of the twentieth century. Sitting right across Silver Creek from the town of Marysville, the huge Drumlummon Mine was only one of a great many other mines, prospects and stamp mills operating in and around the surrounding area. Here's a mild, noninclusive description from *Reports of the Inspectors of Mines and Deputy Inspectors of Mines for the Year Ending November 30th, 1890*:

> [The] *Marysville District is well known for the Drum Lummon, St. Louis, May, Pittsburg, Gold Hill, Louisiana, Bald Butte group, Big Ox group, Carbonate, Gen. Jackson, Empire, Rose Denmore, Mayflower, Uncle Ben, North Star, South Montana, Peggy Ann, Champion, Vanderbilt, Florence, Irish Girl, Bell, Last Hope, Bull and Bear, Johnson, Richmond, Wood-Chopper, Frankia…* [Huff, huff. Catch your breath as there's one more paragraph.]
> *South and west of Drum Lummon are the T.H. Meagher, Bon Mahon, Star of the West, K. of S., Lewis, Montana…Prospect, Marble Heart, Killy, Jeannette, Holland, Robert Emmett, Black Diamond, Marble,*

Little Phil…Grey Eagle, Summit, Rose Cleveland, Intimidation, Atwood, Emma Muller, Hickey, Bluebird, Sanford and White Boy.

Exhaustive as it is, this list contains only the larger registered operations. Between the single-year period of December 1, 1889, and December 1, 1890, the Clerk and Recorder Office of Lewis and Clark County registered 338 quartz claims and 142 placer claims for a total of 480.

Montana mining was exploding at that time. Inspector G.C. Swallow wrote in 1896:

My last report stated there were more than twelve thousand mining claims located and recorded in Montana. But now I can safely say there are more than twice that number.

These returns show the total number of claims recorded in 13 counties during the last year alone to be 8,745. Some of these are doubtless old claims recorded under new names; but the larger part of them are new discoveries. This certainly is a good showing for a state which has had thousands of sharp-eyed prospectors searching every ravine, foot-hill and mountain side for quartz veins during the last quarter of a century.

And keep in mind the list above represents a mere fraction of the total number of mine claims and smaller diggings, all the way down to uncounted single-man prospectors scattered throughout the surrounding slopes, creek drainages and dry gulches. Photos of the time show every scrap of ground in the bustling town site occupied in great mixed crowds of elegant homes, storefronts and hotels to temporary tents and ramshackle cabins. Declarations that Marysville was fast becoming the new Denver of the West were not random boasting but the obvious reasoned conclusion to anybody with eyes.

That 90 percent of that grand metropolis, mines and the infrastructure supporting them is now gone is no barrier to understanding that unthinkable congestion today. All the trees on the surrounding slopes have grown back, yet many only hide still-standing frames of entire homes, mini-ranches, cabins and other structures. Any walk around the edge of town reveals the omnipresent stones piled up in hundreds of overgrown foundation platforms—places where pioneer residents and workers lay claim to their own plot of land for cabin or tent. The old Belmont town site above Marysville reveals so many it looks like the eroding ruins of some expansive, extremely misplaced Roman village.

The true scope of the heyday is mind-boggling.

View from the Marysville side of a now-vanished grand trestle over Silver Creek. Drumlummon is in the background. *Author photo.*

Now forget about the mining industry and just consider the usual vast armies of other people and businesses that come along with not only a thriving boomtown but one of the richest districts in the state. Shopkeepers and merchants of all kinds. Blacksmiths, druggists, doctors and thriving law practices. Liveries. Nearly thirty saloons. Hotels, restaurants, whorehouses and gambling halls. Marysville had a hearty population of Chinese as well, running laundries, shops, their own gambling parlors and opium dens. An opera house and theater. Multiple groceries and butchers. Workers weren't alone, of course, so add schools, churches and a candy shop.

Much of this glut of humanity was compressed into the mile-square Marysville spot, but plenty spilled out into the mountains. Many of the higher mines on and around Mount Belmont had established small mining camp "towns" of their own long before Marysville flourished. Empire. Gould. Gloster. Belmont. Although never springing into true boomtown status—perhaps mostly because of their higher altitudes and further remote locations—a solid dozen or more of these settlements rated legitimate "town" name and status. Unfortunately, the same conditions

Typical—and plentiful—surviving stone foundation platform for tents, shacks and small cabins crowding the hillsides. *Author photo.*

that ensured their eventual dying out also served to more quickly and effectively obliterate what remains.

About 120 years ago, one needed no map. You could navigate by the pounding echoes of the stamp mills or the long march of tramway towers and their constant rumbling trains of ore cars. Scattered cabins, sheds and clusters of work buildings seemed to appear in the background of every old photograph. The growing sprawl of woodsmoke-belching industry and new towns they were birthing was, in nearly every case, as obvious to spot from afar as the glittering towers of the Emerald City. Heck, with a cabin, tent or camp around every rock, asking for directions around here in the nineteenth century would be easier than in a modern mall.

Today, some of those bustling mining camps need GPS confirmation and sworn reassurances from old residents that there was anything whatsoever to random overgrown fields of scattered rocks and charred wood chips. Typically, even less is left of the hundreds—perhaps thousands—of old squatter sheds, work shacks, cabins and other temporary living sites. Ruins of the more substantial kind are still out there, sometimes in locations that make one wonder today how the heck they could ever survive in such extreme places. Many who worked in the mines did not take winters off; so too with the huge support businesses. In the late 1880s, it would be no surprise for quite a population to be scattered in the wild mountains around this busy mining district, as it was not the unpopulated backcountry of today.

There are random tiny grave sites up there, sagging fences still standing around sole tombstones or the eroding markers of a single family. Perhaps these places would have expanded into true cemeteries holding many souls at rest had their boomtowns also expanded. These sites can be so off the twenty-first-century beaten path that it seems more likely the grave is that of the member of an exploring expedition or lost wagon train.

But understanding the relative "high-density neighborhood" of the time helps to better understand some of the GSE reports that still come in from those hunters, hikers and other random travelers throughout the Marysville District's surrounding mountains. And why a puzzling few chose to manifest in the middle of nowhere.

A Furious Phantom

It was a "You should talk to" lead, unsure of exact details but confident this person had encountered a GSE. What exactly had "Mrs. O" really seen? The street rumor sounded pretty good although several trusted sources were not certain. "I think she had a ghost experience in the Red House and/or in the bar [Marysville House]."

Rumor turned out to be half-right as usual yet balanced on that strong base of truth. The story took place not in Marysville but nearby.

Mrs. O didn't live in town but was available via phone. She was another nice, instantly charming personality who was a pleasure to speak to, open to a few surprise questions from a stranger and willing to recount her experience one night at her family's cabin on Deadman Creek, just west of Marysville. And it turned out to be a startling one indeed—a true ghost by any definition. Mrs. O readily agreed with the general GSE theory that it may have been anything from a spooky but natural replay of an event somehow recorded against the background like the Stone Tape Theory to a genuine phantom spirit fully aware and deliberate in its haunting.

"Imagine what I've seen in my lifetime," she told me. "I've gone from horse and buggies to nuclear weapons." As with myself, the longer I live, the more inexplicable the world becomes.

THE CABIN IN QUESTION had stood for many decades before purchase by the "O family." As would later match with Mrs. O's GSE encounter, an "old woman" living by herself was reputed to have been one of the last owners in a long string dating back to the mining days. The woman had passed many years before and died, it is thought, in the cabin itself.

During occasional getaway trips to the new rustic backcountry cabin, "strange things" were beginning to be seen and heard with disturbing regularity—odd noises not natural to their seasoned backcountry ears. These were not pack rats or raccoons but angry, frantic mutterings on the edge of hearing without anyone present to produce or prank. Knockings. Pattering thumps that could be interpreted as bodiless footsteps.

Then there were the unexplainable lights. Bright but compact glows and discreet light sources moving outside in the close woods and around the cabin grounds where remote location, topography and dense forest turned the cabin site on Deadman Creek into a black cave of unrelenting pitch darkness. "It's in the middle of nowhere," Mrs. O. stresses. That meant no city glows in the sky, no gleams of nearby ranches, homes or roads whatsoever beside the rough forest service access track. No summer night hikers with flashlights on nonexistent nearby trails or campgrounds.

Weird, but hardly spooky enough to scare 'em off the property.

THE EVENT THAT WOULD give anybody second thoughts would come in a later warm summer after the new owners had been coming to the place for a while and just started getting comfortable.

Mrs. O was sleeping in a cabin bedroom alone on this—wait for it—dark and quiet night, her husband in the outer common room beyond. What woke her was frighteningly self-evident: the bright glowing form of "an old woman" with long straggly hair and a dragging skirt. "She was all bent over," stooping at the waist and "angrily shuffling from one end of the room to another," where a pair of old beds used to be long ago.

Mrs. O watched from her own bed in a mix of shock, courageously suppressed fright, outright wonder—and a very real regret that her glasses lay just out of reach. Retrieving them would require her to get out of bed and take a couple steps—actions that could break the spell or provoke the apparition's attentions to turn to her. Which seemed like a particularly bad idea the more Mrs. O watched the irate, near-hunchback hag's furious pacing. Whatever raised the hackles of this figure was unknown, but it was clearly broadcasting indignant ire on all frequencies.

"Back and forth, back and forth," a total of three times did this apparition totter, tromp and mutter through its course. It was a manifestation of atypical duration until its total, all-at-once disappearance. And although transparent, imbued with a bright glow of its own essence, the haggard form sported as many "lifelike" details, sounds and movements as a living person. That was powerfully communicated to Mrs. O even without her glasses.

It was enough for Mrs. O to prefer other recreational weekend overnight accommodations, yet she reports her grandson continues to use the cabin as a hunting base camp. "Strange lights and sounds" continue to be seen, heard and talked about.

ANALYSIS AND DISCUSSION

Accurate history of that particular remote cabin is elusive, most down to rumors or years-ago mentions of previous owners and occupants. The report of an old woman who lived and possibly died there is intriguing but lacks a specific name and documentation. These are ultimately just academic details in the face of an encounter with that most prime of GSEs: a full-bodied apparition of sight, sound—and attitude.

The overall impression of a hostile haggard witch woman is also prime spooky, an image as fitting to our cultural ghost mythos as a chain-rattling skeleton. But considering the high numbers of scattered population in the active mining past, it could have arisen from less menacing circumstances. The GSE may be that of an otherwise "sweet old lady," perhaps some miner or teamster's grandmother persuaded for the umpteenth frustrating time to babysit squalling grandchildren while everybody else rode down to the saloons and dance halls. Her angry pacing back and forth? Dispensing homemade poison for all we know, but in pioneer reality probably nothing more sinister than difficulty in getting grandkids in two separate beds to choke down their nightly dose of disgusting castoria.

Justified or not, it's a good reminder for us living folk not to get *too* upset.

For none of us would likely appreciate our temper tantrums getting turned into GSEs and thus earning unfair but sensational titles from later generations such as the Angry Hunchback Hag of Deadman Creek.

CHAPTER 7

DARK CABIN PROLOGUE

CURSE OF WATCHMAN'S ROOST

*That milky vulture eye couldn't seem to decide on which side
of the man's head it wanted to be.*
—*anonymous Marysville resident, 2017*

LATE 1860s
UPPER SILVER, MONTANA TERRITORY

In the blurred, undocumented years before a few ruggedly optimistic prospectors erected the first tentative shacks of the Marysville mining camp, the future town site originally known as Upper Silver was a dangerous, unpleasant place that these tough pioneers took great pains to avoid. Early miners just starting to scratch the surface of the district's great riches routinely detoured around what was then a large fly-infested swamp of rotting jackstraw and stagnant, weed-choked pools. Heavy snow loads lingered in the big pockets between peaks, generating fogbanks of blinding mists through to summers, when clouds of mosquitoes took over. Deadly vipers and poison-spitting toads were believed to thrive throughout the dank, sodden, high-mountain bowl that, come to think of it, would rate a halfway decent rest and staging camp if it ever got cleared out and dried up. Until that happened, the forbidding swamp would be the last place any human in his right mind would choose to reside.

Except for one strange, enigmatic hermit some called the Watchman.

Who was this odd character? Some say he was evil, the Curse of Watchman's Roost solely responsible for violence of the past and the

Rare view of Marysville in the 1870s. *Marysville Pioneer Society.*

powerful supernatural events that linger on the site to this day. Others—like the Watchman himself—claimed he was a guardian against that very evil.

Was the Watchman even human?

His precise name is lost, overtaken by his self-proclaimed Watchman moniker. Most naturally thought that meant he watched the swamp.

There is no written record found, only old, slippery memories of the stories told by a few residents' great-grandparents. Disregard the locality and other specifics, and the Curse of Watchman's Roost could be an ancient European fable rewritten for the American West.

Dark Cabin, however, is quite real, still standing on the supposed Watchman's Roost site and maintained in good repair by the out-of-town family owners. You won't find year-round residents. The family knows better. Any summer visits for barbecues or ATV riding haven't been overnights for years. Rentals have been tried before. None lasted longer than a few months. All refuse to return.

Nothing is wrong with the property or outbuildings. It is a scenic site, grassy with trees. The house is an old renovated cabin but fairly large for its class, in excellent shape and quite livable—if, however, whatever dark forces that give the house its name allow it.

Nobody familiar with Dark Cabin believes that's going to happen anytime soon.

AGAIN I CONFRONT THE problem of over a century and a half of changes.

Yeah, Dark Cabin is sitting there, the epitome of objective evidence. But is the modest promontory of ground upon which it sits the actual Watchman's Roost? This fact is accepted as any other part of the old tale, and 160 years later, it *looks* like it would have been a likely dry spot, slightly elevated above the rest of an imagined swamp.

It was here that the "old hermit" lived in a ramshackle shack that was half wigwam and half lean-to, lodged up against a broken rock outcropping. Not far along the eastern end of this exposed stone shelf was a particularly large boulder, mostly buried but with the top four or five feet above the ground and split in half by a jagged crack. The crack was wide enough for a man to squeeze within had it not been crudely filled in with an overflowing plug of smaller rocks, stones and mud mortar.

This was the Watchman's work and his self-declared reason for existence, why he chose a sole living, struggling to survive the harsh winters and other deprivations of the high mountains. His very presence was an enigma. He was described as a "very old man" in "grizzled clothes almost like ragged robes except for a spotless black, beaver-fur top hat." Wild, snow-white hair and beard. No horse or wagon. No family or friends. He was supposedly established on the edge of the Upper Silver swamp many years before the flood of prospectors. He declared no interest in the new riches believed to be surrounding him on all sides.

A WANDERING EYE

"The Watchman only had one eye…well, a working one, anyway. T'other was all fogged over and milky, creeped out like a movie witch. Probably super cataract. And that was the weird thing about the guy…"

Personally, I believed we passed the "weird" point many miles back, but respect for my elders kept my lips zipped, and I continued to listen to what had to be the strangest thing heard since stepping foot in Marysville. Perhaps Montana as a whole. And that's saying quite a lot. I emphasize I serve merely as the conduit.

"The weird thing was that milky vulture eye couldn't seem to decide on which side of the man's head it wanted to be. The good one and bad one— they kept switching back and forth, left 'n right."

Serious cataracts and other disturbing ocular diseases were the likely historic origin of the so-called vulture or evil eye. As humans are hardwired to regard one another by looking at their eyes—windows to the soul and all that—a milky eye makes it especially disturbing to do so, with all sympathy to the sufferer. The tough prospectors whom the Watchman began to encounter, however, took pity on what they regarded as a crazy old hermit and gifted him with a fine black silk eye patch of which any pirate would be proud.

The patch did not alleviate "the weird thing" about the Watchman's bad eye.

According to the story, nobody could quite agree on *which* eye was bad. For every witness who swore it was the Watchman's *right*, there would be another to swear it was on his *left*. Men would break into argument ten minutes after checking for themselves. Groups in the same visit would disagree. Once when flat-out confronted (paraphrased for sure), the Watchman scoffed at their confusion: "S'simple. I gots *one* good eye and I gots one *bad*."

It's a shame photography of the time wasn't as simple.

No resolution to the debate has survived because it was likely overshadowed by the rest of the weirdness.

The Watchman didn't promote his presence or purpose, but neither did he live up to the literal definition of "hermit." As the mines began opening on Mount Belmont and points beyond, he welcomed the passing prospectors with bitter coffee and frequent shelter. Accommodations were reported to be odoriferous and Neolithic, but his primitive roadhouse was a welcome break along the steep trails and could save your life if you were caught in a sudden storm. The Watchman never charged but eagerly accepted any coin or supply item those passing could afford. Word was that until some trade was offered, the Watchman's conversation would be nothing but thinly veiled hints, although he never turned away the rare person who had less than himself. He never argued or negotiated, accepting the small with the same good grace as the large. The contact with the outside world improved his station, health and mood. In good weather, many would now detour *into* the swamp—or carefully around its toxic edge—for brief rests and visits with the happy old hermit.

The Watchman of the swamp.

Except his presence had nothing to do with the swamp.

The Watchman made no bones about it. Of course, everybody assumed his title derived from a little personal madness and his odd home address. As traffic increased, his honorary role morphed with them and was assumed to include the many trails and growing wagon roads in the canyon. If anybody thought to ask, the Watchman would readily concede he welcomed the rising population and wished them nothing but good. Yet his true duty, his true concern, didn't—*couldn't*—extend fifty yards past his hut and that large cracked boulder.

Because a deadly evil lurked beneath, ever-striving to escape and corrupt all it touched.

Sour Ground

Wishing name withheld (go figure), the anonymous great-grandperson of the early storytellers scoffed, saying the modern retellings diverge at this point into—paraphrased for delicate ears—"a bunch of bunk" about exactly what was supposed to lie far below that crack.

Talk about alternate dimensions and parallel universes only began with science fiction, TV and *The Twilight Zone*. The "portal to Hell" lurking with demons and Satan himself was most popular, most colorful and "most dumb" of them all. The interview subject makes a good point that extends to all similar reports claiming portals to Hell or calling up powerful demons: if you *really* stood on the doorstep to Hell, it ain't likely to be subtle! You'd surely recognize the neighborhood. Hell itself, Land of Eternal Damnation, definitely wouldn't need to post any road signs within miles of its outer sulphur-stench, damned-wailing, flaming suburbs. It is further unlikely that the ultimate Prince of Evil with vast armies of deadly demons would have much problem dealing with a bunch of loose mud-packed stones and a single haggard, one-eyed old man.

Nevertheless, the old story so fragmented today is consistent in the key element that the Watchman's real "job" was gatekeeper against a host of ill-defined "bad stuff" that, if somehow "released" or "allowed to spread," could contaminate, corrupt or otherwise sow seeds of death and destruction.

The Watchman stood alone against the spread of *sour ground*.

The threat profile specifics of "sour ground" are unclear. Traditional references indicate a poor soil or other agricultural deficiency. There's no farming context here, and ironically, the many years of swampy growth resulted in an unusually rich pocket of good soil for the high Rockies once the town site was cleared and drained.

Whatever it was, if the Watchman wasn't on duty, sour ground could spread and lay waste to all around it. There is oddly nothing specific, as if *sour ground* didn't need explanation.

MISSING PERSON

The story ends when Upper Silver's faithful Watchman disappeared one fine summer day.

This fact was supposedly discovered soon after the fact by his many passing friends. "Hundreds" banded together to engage in a great and immediate search. There are conflicting details on time: one has Marysville townsfolk joining in, while another account specifies a somehow "certain and thorough" search of the swamp and its murky waters. There were no suicide notes, blood trails, missing possessions, signs of struggle or other evidence.

Cue a closer look at the cracked boulder. (Note this is supposed to be the top tip of a larger, buried rock with a crack not splitting it in half but rather opening a large fracture leading down into the earth.) There lay a stick of dynamite half buried under a spray of loose muddy stones that had blown or been pushed out of the crack from below.

Uh-oh.

The DVD extra features of this story include a couple alternate endings beyond the theatrical version. So pick your details: a (single shoe/Watchman's hat/eye patch, blood-soaked or not) lay atop the stones, and down alongside the crack's sides were (blood streaks/scrapes of fingernails/blackened soot/torn threads from a beaver hat).

Then far, far below, the shocked searchers heard faint shouting. As if from the bottom of the darkest, deepest mine shaft came the echoing cries of the Watchman screaming out at the tiny silhouettes against the distant sunlight above.

Finishing his job before it was too late ran through all plot lines. Something was trying to get out, but dialogue varied from *it* to *them*. The Watchman's last words besides pleas to blow the dynamite were (a courageous *"I can't hold them back for long!"*/a frightening warning that *"It's almost there!"*/sudden shrieks of agony).

Two versions had the horrified prospectors turn that part of the rocky ridge into a smoking, rubble-packed crater in the time it took to light a match. I like the one where, before they could do so, they were thrown back from a deep explosion and flaming blast that meant the Watchman got to take some bad company along with him.

An unsung hero is gone forever.

The evil for which he stood against and protected us all is safely buried.

Who else wonders why he didn't clue into dynamite or cement mix years earlier?

Lingering Evil?

The sole reason this fantastic tale rates mention is because the "sour ground" of Watchman's Roost is told to be the origin and dark force directly responsible for a host of tragedies over the years and, in modern times, some of the most powerful and frightening GSEs in Marysville.

And why Dark Cabin cannot be occupied by the faint of heart.

Analysis and Discussion

Could "sour ground" be a metaphor for a curse, hex or type of evil spell?

Maybe, had there been some specific mention of anything like that. There's nothing to indicate that one spot of topography had any past tragedy or intense event—no murders, witch burnings, tragic accidents whatsoever to rate what we think of in terms of having a place gain a bad whammy.

Is it pioneer lingo, God forbid, for radioactive contamination? Uranium ores and other radioactive elements were not unknown in the mid-1800s. And while gold and silver were the banner treasures for local prospectors, a nice vein of heavy element could be just as prosperous—if significantly more rare in both occurrence and find. Think you plucked a juicy hunk of uranium ore out of your dusty diggings? Confirmation was pretty simple. A rumored Poor Man's Geiger Counter method of the times was to carry it around in a pocket for a while to see if the tissue beneath got sore.

There is no glowing in the dark, dead trees, grass or plants in the story. The Watchman may have had a bum eye that seemed to dance about between sockets, but there is no reference as a mutant. The sour ground below the boulder was not radioactive.

Was it a biological threat such as a killer virus or germ that could bloom out—say, on airborne spores—spread on the winds and infect plant, man and beast alike with some kind of killer disease? Fits the general suggestion, but thankfully, no all-powerful biological disease entity exists that could terminally infect and then slaughter wholesale populations of animal *and* plant species. But that was the "sense" of the consequences in the story: bad news for *all* living things. "Wasteland" and "snowy desert" were the specific descriptions told to me.

Yet there is no mention of sickness. Only that if *whatever* it was got out to roam free, it would scour all life from the mountains around it. The operational time frame of this mysterious process is always ill-defined with the simple assurance of being too late to fight or stop should it get released.

As the Watchman was never seen in latex gloves or isolation masks—to say nothing of the efficiency of mud-packed rocks that could barely contain chunky salsa, much less a contagious biological hazard—sour ground contains no doomsday diseases.

Sour ground's true nature—if one exists at all—is certain today only in its negative connotation: bad stuff. Not something you want to stumble across in your garden. The Watchman is described as nothing more than an elderly human; not a wizard or magical entity with invisible shields. Therefore, sour ground can be contained or held at bay. Close proximity won't kill you.

A key may lie behind the intent of the story itself. Although only having three available modern sources, each consistent in major details, all three were originally told to them as children and all in the manner of warning them away from dangerous parts of an already-treacherous mining neighborhood. Over staying out too late or committing mischief in the manner of it being a source of vindictive spirits eager to prey on naughty children. Watchman's Roost may be a locally specific version of the ancient "Be good or the Boogeyman'll getcha!" archetype.

Absolutely no documentation has been found confirming any piece of the Watchman story.

NEVERTHELESS, DARK CABIN AND the distinctive ridge upon which it and its weather-beaten outbuildings stand is real. So, too, are the many reports that make the place either foundation-deep in "sour ground" or simply so haunted on its own that it was naturally (if inaccurately) tied to an unrelated myth, as well as several local sensational murders and suicides.

I can see the topographic similarities but nothing to suggest an old pit or "rubble-filled crater." There are no exposed boulders, top tips or otherwise. Then again, I've walked over the overgrown, virtually invisible foundations of entire vanished homesteads in the same area. And all examination of the private property is from curbside gawking.

Credibility point: contrary to my expectations of what should be a kneejerk claim in this suspected western fairy tale, each of the three individuals who would consent to speak denied any suggestion that the Native Americans shunned the area as well. Perhaps that is a completely irrelevant detail, but when it comes to these kinds of stories, native peoples avoiding the supposed "cursed or evil" area is as standard as three-hole punches in notepaper. Accepted without notice or care *unless* they're absent. Or in the case of notepaper, instead of three-hole punches along left side, you find five through the middle.

The origin or authority of the Watchman is also absent—not even a wild guess or wink-wink suggestion of disguised angels or ghosts. This important point is simply not addressed. It's no guarantee, but when it comes to hoaxes, tall tales and other fictions, they're almost always liberally padded with "standard details" such as dark nights, full moons or, in this case, Native Americans shunning the cursed lands.

Furthermore, if exact points like this are asked about without prior mention, the liars or embellishers hurriedly throw them in like forgotten salt in beef stew. *Oh, of course!* Details going against storytelling tradition hint at truth, commonality of specifics or an above-average skill of the storytellers themselves.

CHAPTER 8

DARK CABIN

It was the smiling man, Mommy. The smiling man without a face.
—rumored child of Dark Cabin renters

Potent poltergeists. Self-sparking mirrors hiding mysteries. Invisible sumo wrestlers. Apparitions of classy ladies and furious hags. Phantom echoes of homicidal madness. Houdini light bulbs. Spectral pioneer parades. A startling list of Marysville ghosts and supernatural events that has yet to reach its end. However—at least for now—the town's ultimate GSE superstar stubbornly eludes deep investigation, apparently resisting with a powerful force of its own.

LURKING IN PLAIN SIGHT

The current situation is as frustrating as it is intriguing.

Visitors to France don't ignore the Eiffel Tower. First time in Cairo? Oh, you mean those big pyramidal structures? Funny you noticed 'em. When it comes to rumored supernatural activity in Marysville, Dark Cabin (my term) is the unopened tomb of Pharaoh Tutankhamen. But unlike ancient chambers lost or deliberately hidden under deep desert sands, this "treasure chest" of GSE gems has a specific address, standing there in common knowledge as if supremely confident its haunted reputation will rule the day and protect its secrets.

In fact, the King Tut metaphor may not do it justice. It's rather the Marysville version of the tomb of China's First Emperor Shih Huang Ti (also known as Qin Shi Huang), stuffed with ancient wonders (such as a suspected gargantuan model of the empire at the time, complete with "forever-flowing" rivers of pure mercury and massive torches with enough tar reservoirs to supposedly burn for centuries) and, for researchers, one of the greatest untapped archaeological motherlodes in the world. Ti died in 210 BC. But unlike the modus operandi of Egyptian burials, the First Emperor's tomb is a massive aboveground earthwork edifice with no mystery to a location as well known as any historic tourist site: sprawling under the sun in plain sight outside the city of Xi'an, Lintong District, Province of Shaanxi.

Why unopened after thousands of years? Other than a host of bad spiritual mojo for breaking into tombs that aren't supposed to be broken into—and Shih Huang Ti's is certainly the granddaddy of 'em all, complete with royal curses against any transgressors believed to be perfectly active today—there's far too much cultural reverence and respect to make even its consideration an unspeakable blasphemy.

The proud but comparatively brief legacy of the United States can illustrate this taboo. Imagine allowing any interested parties to take a crowbar to George and Martha Washington's tombs. "Hey, just wanna check things out. No worries. We'll take hi-def photos before we respectfully drag out whatever's left for poking, prodding and whatnot. All for science, y'know. Next week—Honest Abe!"

Why not let Civil War "history buffs" exhume any remaining scraps of prominent generals to highlight reenactments? Assuming some embalming and/or the right mummification conditions, it might be possible to pry legs wide enough to grip a saddle. That, a new hat, liberal pancake makeup and a little duct tape would probably be all that's needed to stage battle charges *with the original commanding officers!* Wow! Instant first prize in the Best Historical Accuracy class.

But of course—and thank heaven—we're as unlikely to see revived Pickett's Charges with George Edward's actual desiccated corpse as we are to see Great President museum exhibits with the genuine-article guests of honor attending as propped-up husks in glass cases. *Still, Marge. Gotta admire those snappy new uniforms. That their real hair?*

As unlikely as opening the tomb of China's First Emperor. *Oh yes, ma'am. We've got them, too. But you'll want to keep going past the snack bar. Hollywood Hall's on your left under the flashing marquee.*

Yet other than the deep respect due any site that represents the hopes, struggles and triumphs of those who have gone before—especially places that have been the home ground of single families down through generations—Dark Cabin is not a national holy ground of untouchable reverence.

Which doesn't mean it can't possess similar powers. Because it dang well seems to actively resist prying eyes and, in my case, noses.

Rumors Denied

When it came to the local GSE rumor mill, Dark Cabin (DC) was prime grist.

In between the shocking reports already related, DC came up time and time again. *That's* the place you ought to check out. *Well, yeah, so-and-so saw a ghost all right, but you should hear what happened over at…*

The place was nice but unoccupied, well maintained by occasional visits of the out-of-town family I had never met. May recall a few summer barbecues over there; a cluster of ATVs and campers? That was all. Fortunately, it was well known enough that I was able to sift through phone book listings and obtain four members of that specific family.

At first I placed a long-distance call across the state to whom I believed to be a family "patriarch" very early on in the meddling snoops—er, investigations. Typically friendly, completely aware of the specific place I was talking about—and quite unaware of any spooky goings-on. I wish he wasn't so sincere, but I wasn't too surprised. It was a major disconnect in the all-rumor data. Typical for these kinds of investigations.

I didn't even bother calling the other three parties.

Failure to Communicate

Angry hags and serial shooters distracted things for a while.

Dark Cabin always loomed in the background like Watchman's Roost, however, perhaps not too unconsciously placed aside as the major subject to tackle. The main details of what rumors I had remained consistent, although by then I was clearly starting to be an annoyance by asking too many questions. Righteous suspicion began to circulate as to what exactly I was going to do with all these sometimes personal town tales.

Time came to reconsider that trio of uncalled numbers from months past.

SUCCESS. OF A SORT.

Things get tricky at this point and remain so today as the first prybars are applied to the truth behind the stories. If there's any hope at proceeding further, this stage requires heightened anonymity: parties are designated simply One, Two and Three. Obviously, they all belong to the same family, all know one another, but it's a rather large clan, and they represent a valid range across a big group.

Call to Number One goes to voicemail. Perhaps ill advisedly, I leave a message.

Call to Number Two gets me a close Cheerful Relative who is remarkably receptive to my strange topic but assures me both Two *and* Three would probably be happy to speak with me. Takes my number.

Call to Number Three rewards me with a live human being. "Hello?"

I know what I can sound like, especially to unsuspecting innocents who bravely answer a stranger's call questioning personal family history. And you can bet I've got a practiced, carefully scripted opener that *usually* reassures the listener on the crackpot factor.

Firm hang-up by the fourth sentence—about the time it took, I now believe, to register the subject of the call and respond as frantically reflexive as getting tossed a hot potato. Maybe some kind of misunderstanding. Not the first time. Question mark next to Number Three for the time being.

There were no call-backs for the next week, and not really expected. People have their own busy lives; my calls may have been unusual but as high priority as returning word to a mattress salesman about a special unsolicited sale. I let half of another week go by and then tried again.

Number One answers right away. Yes, got the message and yes, those rumors are absolutely true. "Just the tip of the iceberg" are a verbatim description and...what's that? No, can barely hear you, either...then a dead line. High-altitude cellphone reception with blocking mountain walls could be problematic at times. Oddly frustrating timing, as there hadn't been a single problem since upgrading my phone eight months before.

Two attempts at redial failed.

"Your call did not go through as dialed. Please check the number—"

Same dang number that's been working fine before. Can't fight tech. Try back later.

As eager to learn more about this "Dark Cabin" as I was to force my phone in line, I didn't hesitate to move on to Number Two. A live answer but another technical foul: the person on the other end was the Cheerful Relative again. Strange timing in calling back; it was only the second time in weeks that Family Member #2 had forgotten that phone! They tried to call you a couple times with this number you gave us (confirms my number) but they insisted you weren't there and may not come back for a while.

Waitasec. "They?"

"Yeah. Or whoever answers your phone. *He.* I think it was a man."

Unless magically stolen and replaced just those times to deflect Two's callbacks, nobody else besides a pair of inarticulate cats has access to my phone. And if it was a wrong number, it had to be a shared wrong number. Somehow.

CR would pass on my call, maybe try again, okay? Oh, by the way, I spoke to Number Three, who'd be *happy* to talk to you. Just call…here's the number. It was the same number retrieved from the phone book and, according to my phone's call log, the same number that had hung up before. I expressed my gratitude to CR for paving the way and pledged to indeed try again if I didn't hear anything myself in a few days.

This second strike was weird if somewhat reassuring that a third try may be a home run, now that my first cold call didn't permanently scare 'em off. Not only that, but a relative had cut through the ice and given me an open invitation.

All I needed was for my phone to work as designed.

THEN THINGS GOT REALLY strange.

A key foundation to my evolving theory of GSEs is that there's no one single process at work, no "unified theory" but multiple phenomena with multiple causes and effects. I extend that to the great variety of UFOs: *if* "they" are visiting Earth, there's also a great variety of spacefaring, dimensionality-hopping aliens, cultures and other quasi-intelligent entities. Okay, if so…

Then I bet some of them have no interest in humans other than to mess with them.

Confusing your cat with birdsong recordings. Throwing two balls to the dog at the same time. Goofy kid stuff, just having fun with the available low-information life forms for a little amusement at their reactions. Complex crop circles with cosmic meaning? More likely there's a saucer in synchronous orbit looking down and laughing off whatever's appropriate to their species.

Of more local concern was whatever forces that play around with cellphones was now mocking me with five solid signal bars, one more than

I had ever seen in that location. It should have been a good omen, but I recall a slight suspicion. Perhaps an unconscious warning that something else besides Murphy's Law might be at work.

Something darker.

I checked Three's number again, carefully hit the right digits with the delicacy of entering a bomb's defusing code. Pressed SEND.

Phone gremlins relented. It worked fine, and I got an answer right away. "Hello?"

"Yes, hello!" I reintroduced myself, asked about the relative's introduction and if it was okay to talk about the Marysville property. "Sure, no problem. Everybody knows about it," was the remembered paraphrased reply. Originally, I had intended to attempt, with permission of course, to record the conversation via speakerphone and a remote microphone on my computer but had decided I'd pushed my technical luck far enough. I was plenty happy I got a working connection with a family lead hopefully about to clear up—or deliver more reports—about this rumored super-haunt.

"That's great to hear. I certainly don't wish to intrude where—"

Click!

Well, it wasn't exactly a "click" with modern phones, but that's the strong traditional expression for "getting hung up on" without so much as a *beat it*. Fair enough had I been cold calling again, but this was ridiculous. Logic demanded another explanation. Number 3 might be wanting to share the call, pressing END instead of SPEAKER—if it wasn't so clearly an early-prefix landline. It definitely wasn't me; I wasn't risking any wrong-button fumble fingers with my phone preset to speaker, sitting open by itself two feet away.

Redialed.

"Hello?"

"Hi, it's me again. Boy, that was weird, I—"

Click!

TIP OF THE ICEBERG

It might take a while, but eventually futility is recognized. At least for this round. Whatever tech snafus were preventing any interviews might put further attempts at risk by annoying the subjects past the point of wanting to bother. That was probably true already; there were no callback attempts by any party the rest of that day and several afterward. I risked it again later that week on a bright, optimistic afternoon. My phone hadn't displayed five bars since that last incident, yet three was just fine. Number One answered, we shared a laugh about the goofy phone service and I was ready for that third-try charm. If I call back…Number One was due at a school sports game, was leaving early and would have extra time waiting in the stands before game time. Half hour okay?

Another delay, but miniscule. I had no appointments and was lucky for an opportunity at all now that gracious Number One had worked it in around other obligations. I gave it an extra thirty minutes and again got through without a problem despite my fears at low signal at this new location or overwhelming background noise. Not so. We could both hear each other.

Finally! I first asked about a pair of specific GSE incidents—not the finer details that would come later but simply whether these spectacular things (further information following) actually happened. The response was a strong affirmative. Not only that but the self-amused, You-Ain't-Seen-Nothing grunt right after was chilling. Like asking a D-day veteran if rumors were correct that storming the Normandy beaches had its difficult aspects. Then came the same phrase, loud and clear, repeated again: "That's just the tip of the iceberg."

"That's a pretty big tip." My phone was in its usual hands-off, speakerphone, critical-call place on desk. Pen held in trembling hand. "What else can you tell me?"

"Hello?"

"Still here. I was asking—"

"I can't hear you anymore. I was saying…hello?"

Oh, no. Not again. Not now! "Yes! I'm here! I—" No use. Again and suddenly without warning, cause or explanation, a phone malfunction torpedoed any telephonic attempt at investigation. You can easily imagine the scene as I yelled and shouted into the phone, listening helplessly—reception in the other direction loud and clear—as Number One asked again and again if I could hear or was still on the line. Number One's phone still ran a connection timer; mine too. According to the displays there was an open, active line. If so, it was one-way, and after another excruciating few seconds, Number One hung up.

Seconds before that happened, I noticed a new status marker I had never before seen on my phone: MUTE.

Somehow, without hands touching the thing from two and a half feet away, my phone decided to engage a never-before-used function to effectively chop off my conversation. Nor is it simple to trigger. I had to refer to the manual to turn it off.

Redial.

"Your call did not go through as dialed. Please check the number—"

TRYING THE SAME THING over and over while expecting different results is supposed to be definitive of insanity. Does that principle extend to things that are specifically designed for and darn-well *supposed* to deliver results different than that which is received? In this case, perseverance was the only plan, but next time let's improve the odds. Strategy called for using a strong, stable landline.

This was a simple thing to arrange, even easier to avoid. While interest in Dark Cabin only grew, I found it easy to keep it on the back burner. I might have been more unsettled at the phone hijinks than I was willing to admit— maybe with good reason with the message I was left a few days later when I genuinely did miss a call.

It was left by none other than the Cheerful Relative, the sole person with whom I was able to have any kind of real conversation during the whole fiasco. It provided no wellsprings of further information or lore but an explanation of sorts. Perhaps a warning as well.

Some family members were having second thoughts at interviews. Not, as feared, because my apparent incompetence with phone devices would reflect my handling of the "common knowledge" stories connected to their family property but rather that "it might be best for me" (note: not necessarily for *them*, but for *me*) if I didn't try any more calls. Traveling to any of their disparate residences might be a time-consuming and costly hassle, but speaking to them personally would be "safer." The distance "a good thing."

Although politely phrased, the implications are clear: whatever powerful force resides in Dark Cabin is actively resisting my attempts at snooping. I'm the one at risk. If I want to know more, I should put a few hundred miles—instead of the current few hundred *yards*—in between myself and the property before asking any more questions.

I've gone too far to bypass or ignore Marysville's GSE Holy Grail, but the next steps need to be carefully considered—as well as the few stunning reports that I managed to confirm (at least in general) as true incidents, even if the finer details remain to be discovered.

BEWARE LOW-FLYING SPATULAS

According to more as yet unsubstantiated lore from the dusty streets of Marysville, Dark Cabin doesn't tolerate unfamiliar occupants such as short-term renters for long. The time frame between move-in and freak-out is one of those previously mentioned unknown finer details. Not-right-away but not-too-long. Sufficient time, at least, for the new unsuspecting victims to become established in the new digs and begin to feel comfortable. Supposedly there were no initial misgivings despite their being fully aware of the haunting rumors. No bad feelings. No negative vibes.

Until the wild flights of kitchen utensils began.

This was no Julian House audio-only kitchen dump. This was a repeated and forceful aerial bombardment of kitchen utensils.

The attack happened sometime around Christmas while the unknown number of occupants were enjoying a holiday video in the living room. Not everybody heard the first light clatters, barely discernible over the TV's cheerful volume. But the rest of the abrupt wood, plastic and metallic storm was unmistakable.

Nobody was in the kitchen to witness this startling debut of flying objects, but all caught sight of various domestic missiles as they hurtled past the doorway. By the time the startled renters got into the room, all the shots had passed. A few spoons, spatulas and wire whisks clattered to the floor— below a frighteningly varied selection of sharper utensils that had embedded themselves up to their handles in the target wall.

Uri Gellar spoon-bending can be entertaining. Occasional bursts of poltergeist activity can be intriguing enough to hang around and learn more.

But all bets are off when it comes to forks, butcher knives and meat cleavers flying through the air with the force of hard-thrown, razor-sharp tomahawks. Spooky now becomes potentially deadly. How can you hope to defend your family against an invisible opponent of such power? There could be no compromise.

The renters left that night.

The typical story variations are included: renters never returned; they refused to ever again step inside and recruited friends to remove their property, even fleeing clear out of state, never to be heard from again, abandoning all possessions as well as (most unbelievable) deposits and months of advanced-paid rent. Worse, these flights of sharp-bladed objects were told to be a chronic problem threatening any tenant or visitor who wasn't a blood relation of the original pioneer family.

Whether GSEs or natural phenomena such as some undetected "sour ground" radiation, it seemed a no-brainer that Dark Cabin could be as hazardous to health as hundred-foot open mine pits. If it was not privately owned, the Bureau of Reclamation would probably have long ago fenced it off with red-letter warnings of "Daylight Approach Only."

So the next logical step?

Renew that *For Rent* listing, of course.

BOUNCING BEDS AND THE GRINNING GHOULS

Too little is known about these last startling manifestations to attempt any dramatization.

The basics are enough to raise anybody's eyebrows.

"Hold on…entire *beds* raising up in the air? *Exorcist*-style? Are you *kidding*?"

"Am I speaking *English*? I don't know about that last part. Nobody's heads spinning around but yeah, you heard it right." Beds—with various children and/or adults occupying them—levitating into the air high enough for violent shakings and jerky rotations.

THE LAST RUMOR CONCERNS the property's outside root cellar that doesn't seem to exist in modern times. Some elements sound suspiciously familiar to an unremembered B-movie plot that eludes searches. It's included only because I *think* it was part of the street-rumored lore yet may not be connected to this particular root cellar or "shadow figure" lurking within.

"It was the smiling man, Mommy. The smiling man without a face." So says the young children who confront this chilling contradiction of terms. Real or imagined, ghostly figures without faces that nonetheless project friendly smiles don't sound like a good thing. Especially when they are reputed to pour on the charm to their uncannily unafraid prey in an attempt to lure them into the root cellar and their ultimate doom.

Er…*okay*.

If this stuff is the tip, I may not want to see the whole iceberg.

ANALYSIS AND DISCUSSION

Show of hands for those who believe these rumors have a serious need for clarification?

Unanimous. What a surprise.

Having a phone or other technical device go haywire is a fact of life. It's nothing new for people. That's what we get for using reverse-engineered alien tech from crashed spaceships before we have full understanding. And while it's true that I hadn't had a problem with making or receiving calls since a move placed me in a better signal location, that doesn't mean the same thing for the numbers I was calling.

While I am no expert on electrical engineering, considering a direct interference by an evil force would also require consideration of a substantial energy transmission powerful and focused enough to affect electronic devices across an estimated quarter-mile distance through any line-of-sight topography and structural obstructions.

So, personal clumsiness mixed with touchy cellphone relays or a supercharged spiritual jamming signal? Lemme think about that for about four seconds. It's an easy conclusion but doesn't yet call for complete dismissal. That's because of a lingering uncertainty about the way even those crazy malfunctions played out. The glitches seemed deliberate.

There's no doubt this situation requires a face-to-face if I'm ever in those other towns and the jamming signals don't move on to my car.

During the brief seconds of good communication possible with the family member, the specific GSEs I asked if true were the flying butcher knives and levitating beds. The stories I had heard were just about "butcher knives," but that has since been clarified to include all types of utensils. There were no casualties.

Levitating beds were also confirmed, although without any other context or extrapolation. There was no time for questions of root cellars for faceless shadow figures; those stories slip back into the Possible Mistaken Myth file for now.

The most intriguing part of it all is that quick and certain "tip of the iceberg" claim.

As much as Occam's Razor reins in our more fantastic explanations, it's also important to remember that reality itself—quite frequently—exceeds our wildest imaginations. The so-called Dark Cabin continues to stand its ground, silent and ageless, its secrets safe.

At least for now.

CHAPTER 9

PERCEPTION PARALYSIS

THE DEMON TROLL OF ASPEN WAY

There's probably nothing on Earth more dangerous to run into.
—Orville Bastian, father of Marilyn Melton

Whil hen investigating GSEs, our best and most convincing tools—our
own senses and perceptions—may also prove the most misleading.
No matter the emotional intensity, we must always keep in mind
that *all* data needs careful consideration before rating true GSE evidence.
Marysville investigations were not exempt from this very human condition,
as demonstrated below.

THE SUDDEN, UNEXPECTED SIGHT froze Marilyn Melton in her steps.

"My knees and legs," she recalled, trembling at the memory, "all felt like
rubber. I couldn't get them to move." She was frightened out of her mind.

With very good reason.

It was a beautiful summer day. Her mother Ruby's birthday, in fact,
triggering lots of wonderful memories. Marilyn went about her normal day,
minding her own business, and then, without warning or provocation—
WHAM! she stumbled across the most dangerous dark entities ever to stalk
the mountain trails above the collapsing ruins of Main Street.

Her very life was at stake. There was absolutely no doubt in her mind: the
next seconds would determine whether or not she was to return alive from
this afternoon stroll in the woods.

And it didn't look good for the home team.

Marilyn Melton, 2019. *Author photo.*

The overgrown slopes above Main Street are home to the best, most visible concentration still left of classic Old West ghost town cabins and residential ruins. Footpaths and trails crisscross and twist about in a dozen courses. Ash piles of scorched glass fragments and black timbers testify to the 1910 devastating fire. Debris, fractured foundations and entire roofless structures give the visitor a vivid idea of how it must have been at the town's busy height. It was certainly a spectacle of Cecil B. DeMille proportions.

In the past, this maze of trails were twenty-four-hour bustling highways of men, women, children, horses, livestock and wagons. Today, they host only the occasional ATV or hiker. For residents like Marilyn Melton, these were paths she hiked all her life. Her familiar backyard.

If your strolling mind happens to wander into the unlikely subject of GSEs on such a bright summer afternoon, then yes, one supposes these trails might prove likely paths on which to encounter a ghost, phantom or other spectral echo of the site's incredibly frenetic past. All those diverse people crammed together over decades around here? Statistics and simple human nature guarantee a good supply of whatever requisite sins, murders, brutal crimes or other evil circumstances were needed for a hearty crop of spooks 'n spirits.

Spooky staircase in "Hill House" above town. It is technically the old home of the G. Kirby family; its nickname comes from its distinct, proud site above Main Street. Safety issues preclude ascent. *Author photo.*

Ironically, on that subject, a pair of fresh graves had appeared only months earlier behind Hill House, the iconic frame cabin ruin perched above Main Street. (Well, to be fair, nobody called it "Hill House" until that new nosy guy moved into town. Technically, it's the old George Kirby place.) And the graves themselves weren't *fresh* in terms of new occupants. The lonely pair of lined rock piles had lost their true natures decades ago until two hand-wrought, iron bar memorial crosses suddenly showed up. Their origins are still unknown and under investigation, confusing even the original family landowners.

Hill House's stalwart, weather-burnt structure stood less than eighty yards away from where Marilyn now stood, knees shaking, wondering if this was the place whereupon she'd join that pair of markers.

While some GSE encounters may be frightening enough that some people could feel they're getting "scared to death," few cases suggest actual physical danger to witnesses. In Marilyn's case, the Demon Troll of Aspen Way was still many hours away from its demonic debut. The "dark, dangerous entities" she now confronted were real-life, flesh-and-blood, claws and teeth.

"On the right side there was a thicket, a crash and a ruckus."

Hill House, the distinctive old home of the Kirby family on a peak of hill above Main Street. *Author photo.*

The mysterious "original" grave markers later replaced by handwrought iron crosses next to Hill House. Even the original landowners/family are reportedly baffled as to their origin. Investigation continues. *Author photo.*

Mama black bear and her two cubs.

"The sow stood up, ten feet away."

Bad circumstances. A sharp turn in the trail, cubs squealing in fright, racing back to several hundred pounds of protective mother with lips already pulling back from quarter-inch fangs. It didn't matter to the admittedly provoked but now snarling monster that the "threat" stood only four-foot eleven and measured her weight in two digits. Bear spray would have been nice, but this was the first bear Marilyn had ever encountered. And even though time had slowed to an excruciating degree, it was unlikely she could have commanded her stunned, trembling limbs to react fast enough.

Or that it would have done much good anyway.

Fortunately, she came back safe and sound to tell her story because when it came down to an attack charge by an angry mother bear, Marilyn Melton could do one better than bear spray.

Make that two.

She had a pair of hiking companions that day: Leroy, her ninety-pound-plus Pyrenees mountain dog, and Princess Jasmine, an unlikely but amazing mix of basset hound and German shepherd manifesting as a stubby, fifty-pound furry log with teeth and a nasty street rep for dirty fighting. Both had been abused in the past, rescued long ago. They were the same pair I'd been babysitting during the Julian House event.

Both leapt ahead in immediate defense of *their* mom.

Everything happened at once. Leroy shot forward, planting himself with splayed legs directly in front of Marilyn, barking furiously. The bear herself had begun her charge but skidded to a hesitant stop. Princess Jasmine's stubby, arm-thick legs were a bit slower, but now she was up flanking Leroy, displaying some serious competition in the bared teeth department and growling menacingly, daring the bear to try anything. *Yeah, I may be only two feet high, but I grew up on the Res, lady!*

"One [dog] would snarl and snap at the bear; she would try and turn to the other one who would snarl and snap....They kept her busy so I could get out of there. I ran on trembling legs."

Mama bear backed down. Backed *up*, to be precise. Then she and her cubs disappeared in the opposite direction with a loud crashing of brush, branches and squealing cubs.

Marilyn Melton is unequivocal: "Leroy and Princess Jasmine saved my life. Very smart dogs."

Good dogs.

"I gave them super amounts of praise and got down on their level, talking to them and thanking them. They also, of course, got some good treats. My dad, ages ago, told me, 'There's probably nothing on Earth more dangerous to run into than a bear sow and cub.'"

That summer saw two family groups of black bears and one grizzly family on the edges and—some nights—right into the heart of town.

"Wow! Are you all right?" I got the preliminary report from her over the phone. I was appalled at the images it conjured up. Thank God she's okay! I'd thought I'd left behind most of the big wildlife in Glacier County. Just when I get complacent, Montana surprises me. Again. Bears were a serious concern past the awe, too, no doubt, but a helluva better one than worries about heavy traffic or crime. Marilyn was concerned they might show up at her house, which was a very good bet considering the three fruit-laden apple trees in her yard.

Montana Fish, Wildlife and Parks responded with a field inspection and suggested installation of several motion-activated lights and noisemakers.

This was reassuring but hardly an ironclad guarantee. That confrontation was justifiably nerve-rattling. Although hardly an expert, I had encountered bears on dozens of occasions and thought her precautions were pretty good. The dogs, of course, remained the best line of defense. Nevertheless, Marilyn worried that any fight might injure or kill them. All valid concerns. "Call me *anytime* and I'll zoom over there, okay?"

"Okay."

THE CALL CAME AFTER midnight the very next night.

The Night of the Demon Troll.

Before that horrible creature showed up, the big concern was that "several" bears were out in Marilyn's yard that very instant, bashing things about on the porch and totally ignoring a frantically barking Leroy at the end of his security chain. Princess Jasmine was inside, nearly drowning out Marilyn in the background, barking, yowling to be let out, outnumbered enemies be damned. Another group of bears (this may have been a single-family group, although fear and darkness made it appear a mass attack) had bulled through the laughable fence reinforcements on the south side and were tearing whole low-lying, apple-laden limbs off the tree with splintering rips.

Marilyn had peeked under a shade and got a growling lunge in return. Now another pair of squealing noisemakers was triggered…she thought they were all running away…

"Holy…I'm on my way!"

I HAD REALLY RESENTED leaving all the drama of East Glacier. But this tiny burg was proving to be far from boring. It was still Montana, complete with weird noises, ghosts and an everyday *Twilight Zone* atmosphere, all in a good way. A place where an idle look out the back window one morning shows the motion that attracted my attention was not a black shadow figure but only Hank, the town's beloved malamute, whose friendly grin resembles a snarling wolf, racing up the street. Hank was wide-eyed scared and running *from* something.

Odd.

The question of what could possibly be chasing such a big friendly dog is a curious one, and the pair of large donkeys galloping into view in hot pursuit was not my first guess. How wonderfully bizarre! Hank got away, no harm done, and now instead of drooling in front of the television I was up racing into the night on an honorable public service. No real worries, either—I had bear spray but planned to stay safe in the car and rely on flashing headlights and a loud horn to scare off any bears.

Except for the broken limbs, scattered apples and other debris, including a greedily consumed wasp trap, Marilyn's yard was empty by the time I arrived. The dogs had calmed down, and nobody was hurt. The bears were gone. Tomorrow would be a day to remove the apples and rebuild fences.

I WAS STILL WIDE awake an hour later. Restless. It was a fairly warm night, so I decided to take a walk, armed with bear spray. But actually, now clued into the many GSE reports, there was more hope for a glowing spirit among one of the many abandoned cabins mixed in with the occupied houses. Considering all the stories that were piling up, late-night walks sounded like a natural duty if I was serious about the subject.

Moonlight and the few streetlights made easy walking on the dirt streets, although deep darkness ruled the forested slopes and tree-crowded yards. I turned down Aspen Way with a passing side mission to make sure the bears didn't return to Marilyn's yard.

I was walking beside that large empty field where the phantom gunshots and faint child cries had been heard. Could the site of that 1896 attempted mass murder really be nearby? My flashlight beam swung over several acres of waist-high grass and weeds. No ghostly gunwomen, no spectral little boy with blood-soaked shirt.

My pace picked up as the field directly to my left began to end with a crowded mass of skinny cottonwoods surrounding another creepy, long-abandoned old house. Had my attention and flashlight beam remained fixed out in that field, I may mercifully have missed the misshapen beast crouching in the brush at the road's edge. Instead, I swept the flashlight back in toward my feet—freezing on the teeth-bared monster barely two feet away.

Scared stiff, indeed.

The flashlight beam was trembling, the only movement on my end as I stood rooted in place. Bear spray was forgotten. So was any useful motor control. My brain shut down my nervous system in a futile attempt to concentrate my full energies on trying to make sense of that…*thing* even now chittering with a menacing alien glee.

I saw a diamond-shaped head. Glaring red eyes—freakin' *huge* eyes, far bigger than looked right even on evil demonic trolls sprouting out side

Marysville street view, 1905. *Marysville Pioneer Society.*

points. Devil-like horns, somehow *twitching* independently like beckoning fingers. I was not sure how that was possible for horns, but its weird, frilled-lizard skull shape deflected shadows.

The teeth had been previously noted, in a great triangular spread that seemed to take up most of the front of the "troll's" head. *Reptilian?* I still couldn't puzzle together the jumbled shape my eyes were seeing. The large tangle of spidery, too-long and too-bent limbs didn't help. Troll? If so, it was a horrific nightmare spider version that went horribly awry in some madman's laboratory. Forget bears. This was hands down the most frightening creature I had ever imagined, and it was *right there*, getting ready to eat me alive while I stood right in front of the dang thing's jaws and—

Suddenly the creature launched itself straight up from its crouch with blurring speed. I stumbled back, arms raising to fend off the teeth-gnashing troll leaping at my neck. Had this strange night actually become the horror movie it appeared, my walk-on role was proving to be brief, dumb and bloody.

ANALYSIS AND DISCUSSION

Perceptual Paralysis—What Did Your Eyes Just Tell You?

Case #1

On a camping trip far up Weasel Creek, my dogs chased some unidentified "creature" up a tree in a nearby draw. Forty feet up and obscured by branches, spreads of cottonwood leaves and the shadows of late twilight, few details of the animal could be made out. It was about the size of a raccoon or skunk but was jet black and seemed not to be crouched on a branch but rather in a *standing* posture next to the tree's thick trunk, hugging it vertically like a tiny little man. That was the creepy element that kicked it out of the ordinary consideration of the usual forest fauna. My weak flashlight beam only made its two huge eyes shine and glare black like mini-headlights. What *was* this mysterious life form?

Case #2

I was walking up on a dark moonless night to check a chicken coop about fifty yards away from the rural home of the owner. Halfway there, I could see the heat lamps were working okay, their orange-red glow reflecting out to one side through a clear acrylic panel. Slight movement attracted attention to the top of a steel fence pole next to the coop. There, somehow impossibly perched on the top of the metal bar, was a barrel-chested dwarf the size of a human child, glaring down at its new prey—me.

Case #3

It was the spring of 2012, while parked along the banks of Two Medicine River east of Glacier National Park, astonished at what I was seeing. I'm no rancher or farmer, but I'm absolutely certain massive black bulls don't normally struggle up against the sky to *stand* on back legs. Yet there it was—barely eighty yards away on an open slope.

Case #4

In 2013, while driving south on Montana Highway 89 as it traversed the vast rolling plains below the Rocky Mountain Front just north of tiny Dupuyer, a dog-sized animal was glimpsed loping away from the road. The impression was not that of a domestic dog, wolf or coyote because its heavy body appeared hairless—not furred but possessing a dark, wrinkled hide. Chupacabra!

"Swear to tell the whole truth and nothing but? Absolutely!" Same situation with GSEs and other inexplicable phenomena or sightings. Consider:

Case #1
The "Creature of Weasel Creek" was only mysterious by a very human failing to identify it and a flash photo that turned its eye reflections red and twice their normal size. Against its dark blob of a featureless body, imagination easily turned it into a sinister—if diminutive—monster. However, easy zoom-in of the digital shot soon revealed the black horn points were actually soft-curved ears. The strange standing posture became as natural as a breeze as eyes could now make out the narrow, lithe body of a black cat hugging the trunk with claws and ready to race higher up the tree trunk.

Case #2
Of all the types of Montana forest wildlife capable of mimicking a stout, evil-eyed troll crouched atop a metal fence pole, the great horned owl is uniquely qualified. It's the largest owl in North America, consistently described by bird guides using terms like *stout*, *heavy* and *very large*. To say it normally reaches lengths of twenty-two to twenty-five inches is problematic without a ruler handy; that means higher than the knees of an average six-foot-tall adult human. Add a thick barrel-like body and hefty ear tufts, and it's a perfect stand-in to trigger wild imagination in low light.

No troll was capable of nearly soundlessly blasting upward to disappear into the night. Once realized, the presence of the owl should have been expected: the chickens inside the coop were clearly visible through the acrylic wall panel. That and the red heat lamps put them on display to any nocturnal predator like a deli counter. The great horned owl (as well as the barn owl) can nail targets from a distance of more than six feet with no more illumination than the equivalent of a single candle flame at a distance of 1,170 feet (0.00000073-foot candlepower).

Case #3
Domestic cattle—especially hefty bulls—do not rise up on their hind legs. Bears, however, are well known to do so with relative ease, and that's exactly what this giant, cinnamon-phase black bear was doing. It seemed anxious and suspicious of the small strip of Highway 49 between it and the Two Medicine River and was standing, as is believed by bear researchers, simply to get a better look. Why the first impression of a

standing bull? Despite the raw data my eyes were clearly offering, my brain insisted on turning bear to cattle because of the modest herd of big, black free-range cattle that had been grazing on that same hillside earlier that day.

Case #4

"So…um, you say there's been no recent reports of chupacabras or other weird beasts running around Teton or Pondera Counties?"

"No, sir. Not there or from anywhere else." The lady at the Montana Fish, Wildlife and Parks office was polite, helpful—and nice enough to save any laughter until after the crackpot's phone call. "As far as 'recent' goes, I can assure you that we've *never* had any reports of that nature."

Well, you never know. As my report wasn't among a slew of other strange sightings along the Rocky Mountain Front, I can safely assume with my track record that what I spotted was more likely a mangy coyote or stray dog than a chupacabra.

The "Demon Troll" Revealed

Scientific name: *Odocoileus hemionus*. Or, as more commonly known: mule deer. Probably a yearling or small adult. *Certainly* one that was startled as badly as I was. It was a classic case of being in the wrong place at the wrong time for both species. For the mulie, it was an unfortunate choice of thick brush near the road to bed down for the night. The human's contributing mistake was wandering around in the dead of night with a specific mindset of ghosts, ghoulies and monsters.

What if, for instance, it *had* been a lingering bear with a foul taste for surprise instead of a freaked-out mule deer frantically levering up on its scaffold of thin legs to bound off at top speed? Game over, indeed. The mulie crashed off. Silence returned to Aspen Way. And a good minute and a half passed before my knees unlocked, my breath returned and my brain rebooted.

The point is that human perceptions are slippery and incredibly susceptible to the power of suggestion. Especially as any bias arises out of one's own mind, this characteristic can be especially problematic when dealing with the sensory data of the strange or unusual. GSEs are the very epitome of strange and unusual.

When can you be sure of what your physical senses are telling you? All contexts must be considered as well as the sum total of objective evidence—if any—available. Normal human nature. We all know the examples—as anybody in law enforcement will confirm—of the inherent unreliability of eyewitness accounts. You can't help what you *think* you heard, saw or felt, but any investigator must realize even the most heartfelt belief can be flawed through no fault of the witness.

The previous case examples of my own mistaken identities, taken separately and out of this context, can be mildly amusing anecdotes on a clueless Midwest flatlander confronting the wild wonders of the Rocky Mountains. But regardless of the simple truths behind them, initial impressions *swore* otherwise.

I've made *waaay* too many mistakes by now to instantly accept the fantastic. I believe this fundamental attitude contributes to the brainfreeze, trying all that much harder to squeeze garden-variety meaning into the *Twilight Zone* impossibility I *think* is unfolding past my nose. Also, in most instances, photographic evidence or simply hanging around long enough to figure it out eventually revealed the truth. The "chupacabra" sighting is the sole exception but nonetheless discounted through sheer unlikelihood.

However, had circumstances somehow removed me before the opportunity to sort it out (like having sufficient reflexes to immediately turn around and beat feet), I'd have a completely different story to tell. (This also assumes a level of normal human stubborn ignorance and a total inability to figure out/admit to a real-life alternative. Y'know, a characteristic to be found in virtually every person walking around today.) If forced to give solemn testimony under oath in a court of law, I would have had no choice but to admit that yes, I know how it sounds, but chipmunks ain't the only wildlife out there. I've seen chupacabras, pirouetting Brahma bulls, pole-sitting dwarves and demon trolls with five-inch fangs.

ORVILLE BASTIAN SPEAKS TRUTH, but it's ultimately a problematic exercise when attempting to gauge the "most dangerous" animal one may encounter in North American forests. Technically, most modern wildlife experts consider the moose—largest of the deer family—to be the "most dangerous." Frequently approaching one thousand pounds with antlers that could have an eight-foot spread, an angry moose offers an opponent a ferocious temper, greater height and sometimes twice the mass of an average sow bear. Yet comparisons are like trying to qualify the difference between stepping into the path of a speeding truck versus a speeding bus. The end result is pretty much the same.

Soon after I arrived in Montana in the 1980s, a friend told the story of a large Schwann's truck forced to brake to a stop because a huge bull moose had decided to stake out that lane of highway just west of Helena. A few minutes of silent standoff, and then the driver decided to scare it off with a blast of his air horn. Bad idea. The moose instantly attacked, pummeling the front of the truck with its huge, sharp antlers. The driver struggled for the clutch and gearshift, cab rocking violently with each titanic slam. Before he could get his truck in reverse, the engine seized as metal squealed, grill ripping apart, whole foot-long pieces of steel safety bars blowing inward to collide with the spinning fan assembly. The last sight of the moose was through the haze billowing out from the ruptured radiator: unhurt, giving an annoyed snort and slow saunter off the highway into the trees, confident of its victory.

Elsewhere on Idaho's Clearwater River, six foolish lumber cutters in a sturdy wooden boat spotted a swimming moose and decided to bag it as dinner, attacking with their axes. Despite a water depth over its head as well as a fast current, the moose fought back, killing two of the lumberjacks and destroying the boat.

CHAPTER 10

POSSIBLE GSE TRIGGER EVENTS FROM THE PAST

And with this dull blade he sawed the tissues of his neck…
—the Mountaineer, *September 22, 1904*

As distinctive as Marysville's history may be, many aspects are shared by virtually every other place on Earth where there is—or has been—a high concentration of people in residence. Given enough time, enough people and enough real life, the vast majority of small towns will eventually accumulate their share of good *and* bad happenings. Triumphs and tragedies. Near-misses and deadly freak accidents. Great charitable displays along with assaults and hot-blooded homicides.

Pump up the emotional intensity—such as over five thousand people overflowing a single square-mile mountain valley of rumbling railroads, gigantic stamp mills pounding away 24/7, smoke-belching industry and the bustling Wild West metropolis right at the heart of it all—and then yes, some drama should be expected to crop up here and there.

The other half of this formula has nothing to do with human nature but the sheer number of moving parts in constant chaotic motion. Person, livestock or machine, sooner or later there's going to be argument and accident. Reality, pure and simple.

So as this chapter focuses on past local dramas of various types, it's within the context of seeking out specific incidents from history that may be associated with the manifestation of ghosts and/or supernatural events. It is not a reflection of the town's overall positive and thriving character throughout the years, only the admittedly sensational, negative turns of fate that may be relative to the current popular theories for triggering GSEs.

The cases dealt with here are both well documented and far enough back in time as to have, to my knowledge, little to no active connection to any current residents. Nevertheless, it is never forgotten that these are the accounts of real people who hopefully now rest quietly. Or does final peace elude some tortured souls? Are any responsible for the GSE reports?

1883—Wrong Place, Wrong Time

Shortcuts save time. But as we all know since childhood fairy tales, these can be dangerous routes.

For John Duffy, engineer at a twenty-stamp mill at the nearby Gloster mine, his unfortunate choice of shortcut shaved nothing but time off his life.

Nobody short of those with a death wish *intends* to have whatever accidents befall them. Duffy wasn't intending anything but a quicker trip to his dinner. But he did not take the long way around and fatefully chose to use the mine's elevated tramway as his shortcut, only to be caught in the path of a fully loaded ore car descending at full speed.

An ultimate wrong place/wrong time situation.

Gloster mining camp. *Marysville Pioneer Society.*

The risk Duffy took can't be fairly judged because of the choice of words used between the May 9, 1883 *Helena Independent* and the May 11 Butte *Daily Miner* newspapers. The latter stated Duffy was "crossing the tramway on his way from the engine house to his dinner" (the modern equivalent of dashing across a street to beat traffic) or "walking on the tramway" in the former's report—as if strolling along the same highway in the middle of busy traffic.

Context suggests Duffy was in danger's path longer than a quick dash, apparently walking downhill and unaware of the ore car's approach from farther up the line until the last few seconds. A panicked slip took away his last chance at leaping out of the way in time, the speeding ore car catching and crushing his right thigh. Poor Duffy was not granted the final mercy of a quick death, yet his last agonizing time on Earth was spent in great worry not for himself but for "an aged mother in Indiana who was dependent upon his earnings for support, and about whose welfare he was chiefly concerned about during his dying moments," according to the *Daily Miner*.

CIRCA 1890s—NOT ALWAYS THE BEST MEDICINE

The timeframe around this startling and enigmatic stray photo in the Pioneer Museum is an estimate from background details. Here in splendid top hat, long tails and royal finery stands a tall black man with chiseled features. Logic suggests he'd be better known than the simple "Mr. Brown" label, but so far he has left no other legacy (yet) than a few old typewritten lines of his unusual fate from an unattributed author: "Found a quarter while swamping out Dinny [sic? Danny] Shea's saloon—developed a fit of laughter over it and died."

Not a bad way to go, although tragic he didn't get to spend that quarter first. And modern medical science suggests it wasn't the mirth itself but a lurking health time bomb like a heart attack, stroke or aneurysm that was merely set off by what must have been a real belly-shaker.

1894—A FATAL FEUD

Interred at the Marysville cemetery with one of the few surviving monuments, Hans E. Thompson was not a resident within town limits.

He and a man named Van Fleet lived on Thompson's ranch about eight miles away, according to the *Mountaineer* of March 29, 1894, "at the upper end of what is know[n] as the Little Valley, at the headwaters of the Little Prickly Pear."

Unfortunately, "just across the stream from this ranch" lived the Ford brothers: Ben (Benjamin) S. and Augustus W. Ford. As if typecast outlaws from an old western, this nefarious pair were portrayed as heavy-drinking, irresponsible thugs. There had been a long-simmering feud between the two ranches, Thompson frequently complaining of the Fords "encroaching" on his land. "The Ford boys threatened more than once to take the land belonging to the other parties."

The Ford brothers arrived in town on the morning of March 25, 1895, and hit the saloons, and by 11:30 a.m., they were reported to be "fighting drunk." They were suddenly in the mood to settle the border conflict once and for all and made no excuses when purchasing ammunition for their Winchester rifle and setting out for the adjoining ranches.

On the way, the *Mountaineer* reported that the Fords met Van Fleet on his way into town and flat-out told him they were on their way to kill Thompson. It's not noted why Van Fleet wasn't assaulted nor did anything to stop them when they met on the trail. Outnumbered and possibly unarmed, he likely had no choice but to continue into Marysville to alert authorities. Furious "fighting drunk" brothers with a firearm? Van Fleet gets the benefit of the doubt. At any rate, enough time passed between the encounter and Van Fleet's return to the cabin to discover the threat fulfilled: Thompson dead of a rifle shot to the chest.

The Ford brothers were ultimately acquitted, but neither enjoyed happy lives thereafter.

1897–A BAD BET

Today, it's a tangled mess of vegetation and beaver dams.

In 1897, it was a large millpond.

May 23 of that year was reported to be a Sunday—probably meaning a spring day off that accounted for the "number of people" supposed to be...dare I say *milling* about at the edge of the pond. It must have been a warm day as well, helping to bolster thirty-five-year-old John Leidler's courage. He boldly bet the crowd that he could swim the millpond's entire

Marysville millpond site today. *Author photo.*

An early Marysville view labeled "Wood Yard and Many First Residences." *Marysville Pioneer Society.*

length underwater "and at once proceeded to demonstrate the assertion," according to the *Mountaineer* of May 27, 1897.

Leidler never made it.

The top of his bobbing head was seen early in his attempt, but he failed to surface. Time continued to pass without a ripple, and soon the bystanders became an impromptu search-and-rescue team, many jumping in on their own accord and requiring multiple dives to finally recover Leidler's lifeless body "some distance from the starting place."

Apparently, Leidler didn't drown. The explanation sounds forensically shaky today: "A medical examination showed that when he struck the water he broke a blood vessel, death being caused therein." Nevertheless, dead is dead, and becoming so under tragic circumstances is supposed to be a key formula for GSE manifestation. John Leidler was Cornish and had moved in barely two months previously yet earned many friends in that short time. He was buried in the Marysville cemetery the day after the accident. His exact grave spot is as lost as most others.

December 1899–A "Terrible Death"

"Terrible" is an accurate term in how the *Mountaineer* of January 5, 1899, describes the end of John Harrington, a local "old timer," in a cabin seven miles south of Marysville, a half mile below the Big Ox mine. Indeed, getting torched to death while your cabin burns up around you is high on most people's Hope Never Happens to Me lists.

The newspaper portrays Harrington as a bit of a hermit. He had lived by himself for several years, selling garden goods and dairy products from a few cows. Harrington was "an old man with some peculiarities, and the neighbors did not know him well." Rumor had it he had not gone to town (Marysville) in three years.

Hermit or not, he still had neighbors close enough to notice the fire and concerned enough to respond. But it was too late—Harrington's cabin was fully engulfed, and a roof collapse cut off any rescue attempt. They had to wait two days before the smoldering ruins allowed a close approach.

Searchers found little to recover: "A portion of his skull and some teeth, his body even to the remainder of the skeleton having been destroyed by the flames." A later inquest held by Acting Coroner Steinmetz ended up with "the usual verdict" by the jury, meaning there was no sign of foul play and circumstances were determined to be exactly what they appeared: though specific means impossible to define, old man John Harrington burned up with his cabin. Who knows? Smoking in bed, knocking over a hot stove or stumbling into an oil lamp during a fatal stroke or heart attack, whatever caused the fire was likely an accident. Further evidence that the man was subject to epileptic seizures only bolstered the verdict.

1900–KILLER MELANCHOLY IN BELMONT

Belmont was one of those mining camps that, depending on the ever-fickle roll of economic fortunes, could have risen to a modern town in its own right but now exists only in old faded photographs. Belmont was a close neighbor in 1900, and the unfortunate soul in this case—Sophia Anderson—has been laid to rest in the Marysville cemetery.

On March 16 of that year, thirty-seven-year-old Mrs. Anderson, according to the county coroner inquest, "came to her death…by means of carbolic acid poisoning, administered by her own hand while in a state of melancholia." She deliberately drank the corrosive toxin right out of the bottle.

Suicide is incredibly distressing in every way to every ear. The desperate choices those despairing souls chose more than a century before can affect our living hearts today. And if anybody is curious about what "melancholia" may feel like, there is no need to go further than Sophia's stone cemetery marker.

In further distinction: of all the estimated "many dozens" (own estimation through various references) of grave sites in that cemetery, the exact locations of which have been erased by the high-altitude Rocky Mountain weather, Sophia Anderson's marker stands strong among the few tombstones that survive. It is a sad testament to both the terrible black power of bad mental health and the ultimate senseless waste of the act of suicide in itself. The medical state-of-the-art for such things in 1900 was not in the poor woman's favor. Tragic as it was that her inner turmoil forced her into a horrific act, it's possible some good may arise if only one other person at risk recognizes the futility of Sophia's choice and makes a positive, completely opposite choice of their own.

1901–A DELIBERATE DIVE OF DESPONDENCY

The millpond claimed its second victim less than four years after John Leidler's death. It was no accident this time—unless poor Hazel Mather miscalculated in making her fourth attempt at suicide the real deal when she threw herself in the deep millpond on the evening of April 24, 1901.

A pitifully young twenty-seven years of age, Mather's troubles were deemed to be caused by troubled romance. To an extreme degree. In fact, she is clearly labeled by the May 25, 1901 *Anaconda Standard* as "a demimonde of Marysville" and—

Oh, excuse me. A "demimonde"? I did a double-take and had to look that one up, too. And when I did, I thought Mather may have had a better cause for a slander suit than killing herself. Pick any one of the definitions offered by trusty Webster's: "the class of women who have lost social standing because of sexual promiscuity," "prostitutes as a group" or simply "any group whose activities are ethically questionable."

Chinese District overlook. Picnic Hill looking up Marysville Road as it rises toward the Great Divide Ski Area. *Author photo.*

Her actual leap into the deep industrial millpond was not witnessed, but the (unnamed) mill engineer on duty at about ten o'clock that evening had no doubt what had happened. He had just noticed the odd sight of the woman standing at the edge when duties briefly distracted his attention. He glanced back only a few seconds later and could no longer see the woman. Nobody could have moved out of the visible open ground in that time unless they went into the water.

The engineer didn't hesitate to race down to the area, distressed to find big splash puddles. Despite immediate rescue efforts, Mather's body eluded recovery until mid-afternoon of the next day. It was obviously another case of a whole town well aware of a resident's troubled life. The tragic outcome was deemed clear; there were no signs of foul play, and Coroner Brooke declared no need for a formal inquest.

What pushed Hazel Mather into taking her life that night? What was the always-suspected, always-searched-for climatic trigger event? A specific reason is not clear. A day after the event, the *Anaconda Standard* reported that Hazel "had a row with her lover and said something about suicide," the next day declaring she had "committed the deed in a fit of jealousy." This contrasts with reports only the day before from the *Helena Independent* that "it was not known what prompted her to drown herself."

You can bet the rumor mills were spinning. Adding special spice to the mix was the high drama of not long before, when Hazel decided gunfire was the best option in a disagreement with then-boyfriend Joseph Luxton.

That was March 1900 (depending on how you interpret old paper references), when Hazel Mather was arrested on a first-degree assault charge. She and Luxton alike were fortunate that wasn't first-degree murder. It may well have been *attempted* murder had not the spark of love yet burned between the parties and "the wound was not a dangerous one," according to the *Helena Independent* of April 25, 1901. The charges were dropped to second-degree assault. Luxton soon recovered.

Move forward a few months to a June 5, 1900 *Anaconda Standard* reporting that Mather has been in custody at the Lewis and Clark County Jail in lieu of failure to pay fines of "$360 and costs" with 120 days left to serve. However, the real news was that Governor Smith responded to an appeal by the sheriff to reduce Hazel's sentence because of an affliction of rheumatism and that she be allowed to return home to Marysville and the care of friends. "Costs" were never specified in the articles, but Smith forgave all but $200. This remainder was raised either by a combined effort of Marysville neighbors, according to the *Anaconda Standard* of June 5, 1900, or Luxton all by himself, as suggested by the *Helena Independent* rehash a year later on April 25, 1901.

This incident is important because it shows—on the surface, at least—that Hazel always had friends. Somebody(s) raised her bail. She had a home to which she could return. Her relationship with Luxton was contentious, with only imagination to define the scope. But he didn't cut off all ties after a little blood-spilling gunplay. New jealousy may have been enough of a motivation. It's down to that inevitable *who knows?*

In a GSE context, it's a classic Woman in White narrative—a despondent soul throwing herself to her death because of a broken heart. Might her despairing spirit yet roam?

1904—PRIDE GOES BEFORE THE BLADE

According to Marysville newspaper the *Mountaineer* of September 22, 1904, resident John W. Jones had "previously borne a good reputation as far as his honesty was concerned." The "about 50 years of age" man was noted to have been unemployed for several years except for odd jobs like "swamping out" (mopping and cleaning) saloons—until the day Charles Peabody swore out an arrest warrant, accusing Jones of "having broken in and robbed the money drawer in his saloon of ten dollars." Constable Middlebrook soon had Jones behind bars.

Both the *Mountaineer* and *Anaconda Standard* reported the story but give contradicting times for the critical event: *Standard* says "breakfast," while *Mountaineer* says "dinner." These are perhaps inconsequential details in the face of the clear fact that, no matter what meal was being served, John Jones took advantage of the knife that came with it to cut his own neck.

Twice.

This wasn't in the manner of a bloody horror-movie throat slash. In some ways, it was worse. Cutting one's own throat requires only desperate determination and sufficient coordination. The instant drop of blood pressure and other terminal, no-argument physical factors guarantee a singular action resulting in quick death.

John Jones chose a more horrific method, perhaps forced to do so by the limited efficacy of the only tools at hand. The *Mountaineer* reports the gruesome details: "On the tray containing his meal was a table knife, and with this dull blade he sawed the tissues of his neck until he severed the arteries and veins on both sides of his windpipe. After cutting his throat he lay down on the bed, covered himself over with the clothes and seemingly died without a struggle."

County coroner A.P. Yeager investigated the tragic incident and conceded no inquest was necessary. Jones left a note insisting he was innocent but "did not feel he could endure the disgrace of his arrest." John W. Jones was to be buried at Marysville.

Could Mr. Jones have had more to worry about than damaged pride from a false accusation? The news reports noted "at the time of his arrest money answering in the main the description of the denomination of that which was stolen from the saloon was found on his person." Sounds like damning circumstantial evidence, but what exactly is meant by "answering in the main the description" of the stolen loot? Ten bucks was stolen and Jones had two fives? A fiver and five singles? It was all green? It doesn't sound like an accusation of having *the same exact bills* somehow known as stolen. Yet I believe this had more credence than it would today in a modern courtroom. Jones's life circumstances were well known; he did not sound prosperous in any way. This may be akin to cops responding to a burglary report of $200 stolen from a house and then finding ten twenties in possession of a familiar penniless transient camping nearby. Jones's explanation of recent pay for ranch work

The unburied bones of one of Marysville's many thriving businesses. *Author photo.*

was given no weight whatsoever. There should have been no problem in verifying the ranch story, and it was likely attempted without success.

Jones was probably guilty.

He was definitely aware no saloon owner would trust him again. No more swamping gigs, and other likely local employment may have been impossible for his circumstances and/or reputation. And if defending his name was really that important, the ranch work pay could not be impossible to verify, especially if were a valid alibi against a theft charge. Jones should have been the first one to indignantly lead deputies to this phantom ranch. And even fearing conviction for what ultimately would be a false accusation, was that enough for which to throw away your whole life? I'm unversed on the 1904 criminal code but doubt a ten-dollar theft would land one in a maximum-security penitentiary. For a despondent Jones, the ripple-effect consequences were enough. The desperate actions speak for themselves.

May 12, 1907—Deadly Domestic Dispute at Bald Butte

The Bald Butte mine and town site is located about four or five miles from Marysville, up "over the hill" (Mount Belmont) on the western slope of the Continental Divide. Although a good producer of gold-veined quartz during its early years, it was considered pretty much worked out by 1866. Production dropped, and the owners decided to close both the mine and its ten-stamp mill. But soon thereafter, the discovery of a new ore body ledge brought Bald Butte out of early retirement. The mine continued to operate until the Bald Butte Company finally closed up shop in 1917.

Both town and mine were still bustling in 1907—perhaps overcrowded to the point of triggering homicidal tempers. The specific affront that caused (unknown age) George Melvill to fatally stab his roommate with "a long-bladed hunting knife" was never admitted by the killer. Did a housing shortage for Bald Butte's many workers contribute to the murder of thirty-nine-year-old Winfield Clark "W.C." Guthrie? Some kind of domestic disturbance that got out of hand? "Presumed to Be Result of Family Quarrel" declares the local headline.

The *Helena Independent* of May 13, 1907, reports what seems to be an unusual living situation: two families sharing the same home. Maybe overcrowding made that a common necessity with limited worker housing throughout the busy industrial beehive of the Marysville Mining District.

Bald Butte. *Marysville Pioneer Society.*

Whatever the circumstances forcing a shared address, the different parties had better get along.

"Both men have been working in the Bald Butte mine. Guthrie is a widower with two children and Melville [*sic*] is married but has no children. Both families have been occupying the same quarters at Bald Butte and were seemingly 'on the best of terms.'" In this case, things seemed to be working out.

Until the night Melvill turned killer.

Marysville physician W.A. Peek examined the body and agreed with witnesses that Guthrie certainly died within ten minutes, bleeding out from the severing of major blood vessels from the large knife wound on the left side of his chest below the collarbone.

Melvill didn't lift a finger to hide his deadly deed. Details are lacking as to how the Bald Butte mine superintendent John Edgerton found out about the killing, but it is presumed that neighbors, Guthrie's children and/or Melvill's wife (who witnessed the whole thing) alerted others. It was Edgerton who telephoned Marysville requesting the constable.

Melvill also made no attempt at eluding law enforcement. He was "collected enough to be able to eat supper" and then waited "coolly for the arrival of the officers."

No reason or excuse was given.

1917–IN THE LINE OF DUTY: VALMORE DEROSIER

The value and meaning of those lost to a family and community—
especially those who voluntarily put themselves up to protect that family and
community—can never be reconciled against the crime or criminals that take
them away. It is no surprise then that the *Montana Record Herald* of September
13, 1917, describes Marysville constable Valmore "Val" DeRosier as "one
of the best known men in Lewis and Clark County.…[He was] repeatedly
elected constable and rendered very efficient service.…Marysville was never
so wrought up as she is today over the terrible crime that has cast a pall over
the entire community."

This is the story the *Record-Herald* describes:

About eight o'clock the Thursday evening before, DeRosier was patrolling
the streets when he met up with Dan Shea, foreman of the St. Louis mine,
who was returning home from his work shift. As they stood there enjoying
the evening and a friendly talk, both were startled by a "muffled" but
unmistakable explosive blast.

Startled, they looked around. There were no smoke plumes, debris or hint
of fire in sight. There were no mine whistles or alarm horns announcing
trouble in the tunnels either, but each felt sure whatever it was had been
very close, much closer than the mines. Shea joined his constable friend in
a check of the business district. DeRosier used his flashlight to check for
interior damage through the shop windows, while Shea made sure doors
were locked. Nothing amiss on the first bank of shops and mercantiles. The
pair crossed over Main Street and began working back on that side.

On approach to a dark corner of Nels Lund's saloon, a loud "Hey!" was
shouted out of the blackness. DeRosier turned, and the ambush-attacker
fired a bullet that shattered the flashlight and passed through DeRosier's
hand and into his abdomen. Wounded and bleeding, he ran north while
an unarmed Shea bolted south. "Robbers" (later context states a "pair")
jumped out of the darkness and fired "12 or 15 shots in quick succession"
at Shea, who, with hot slugs whizzing by his head, "sought entrance to
[probable translation: frantically kicked in door of] a store on the opposite
side of the street."

Constable DeRosier succumbed in the street from his wounds. Dan Shea
escaped, but so did the murderous "yeggmen," criminals with the specialties
of burglary and/or safecracking. An accurate description of the crime:
the saloon safe had indeed been blown open but with a senseless-for-all-
concerned ultimate haul of only twelve dollars. Authorities believed this was

the work of a gang that had been doing the same thing in East Helena, timing their robberies with large reserves to cover paydays. The payday at the mines was due, but apparently the thieves were unaware of which saloons had the best cash caches.

MINE ACCIDENTS

Industrial accidents large and small are going to happen wherever people and bustling industry mix. The Marysville Mining District was no exception. The district had its share of fatal mishaps but fortunately none of the large-scale, mass-casualty disasters that have occurred elsewhere. Yet over the years there would always be some miners who never made it back alive from their work shifts.

Just about all of these accidents, by their very nature, are "dramatically intense" as assumed GSE trigger events. Shaft falls and premature

Mystery generic miner photo reveals unknown presence of women in one of the many mines throughout the district. *Marysville Pioneer Society.*

explosions—none of it is pretty and, for investigative purposes, wholly moot. One early 1900s account swears sighting a so-called tommyknocker. But if GSE manifestations are limited to occurrence sites then any lingering phantoms are haunting lightless abandoned tunnels, likely flooded to the roof if not collapsed long ago.

As definitive as mining is to the district and town of Marysville—as well as most of these GSE reports—the heart of the industry, the mines themselves, are not part of this investigation.

At least *not now*.

CHAPTER 11

RANDOM REPORTS, FUTURE COURSE AND THE GREAT 2018 TEAM INVESTIGATION

WHERE DO WE GO FROM HERE?

Searching for ghosts? Just look around. Up here they're all around us.
—paraphrased from multiple Marysville residents, October 2017

The vast majority of these GSE reports are established Marysville "common knowledge" lore. But sprinkled between the more spectacular and well-known events are several random notes of unsubstantiated, single-source ghost sightings that have yet to rate local confirmation.

One of the most intriguing involves the apparition of a headless woman haunting one of the town's homes or outbuildings. Somewhere along the line, this report was confused with the Angry Hunchback Hag of Deadman Creek, and Ms. O's witness confirmed the error. Apparently, my imagined personal secretary failed to tag specific sources, and so far this headless woman ghost remains a rumor. However, confidence lingers that this is indeed another valid Marysville ghost report just waiting to be revealed.

NET LUNACY

The few so-called ghost sightings found on the Internet are immediately suspicious. In fact, little to none can be found. The bulk are from the website Legends of America (legendsofamerica.com/mt/marysville) and sound patently absurd, as if dropped in from a random list of spook archetypes to merely fill up the spirit sightings box on that particular page. These include the ghost of a headless miner "near 1 Spring" and another phantom miner (this one *with* his head) with "big mustache and hook hand," as well as a headless woman wandering around up on Mount Belmont. Again, the headless woman here is not to be confused with the *in-town* headless woman report I believe is more credible.

Locals suggest many ghosts have been seen throughout the forests of the district, but none had heard of the specific details offered. Nobody I asked has heard of "1 Spring" (with attendant phantom miner, headless or not), and a ghost miner with a big 'stache and hook for a hand sounds too formulaic. Campfire tale cliché. If Marysville was a coastal fishing village, there would be sightings of a *sailor* with a big mustache and hooked hand.

A final "ghost sighting" is so ridiculous that it has to be hoax or outright filler-box fiction: "Near Marysville, an unexplainable hunter, who is riding a bicycle and appears to be severely mangled has been sighted pulling a dead wolf."

Here was the scene in the Marysville House bar: "Say, fellas. Any of you guys ever hear about the ghost of some mangled-up, bicycle-riding hunter pulling a dead wolf?" Same grins and confident denials from every other resident I dared ask. That meant it was virtually impossible such a thing was ever seen in the area. Absolutely zero hits on other searches—which, as we all know, doesn't guarantee a valid report exists—but when it comes to Internet search terms, "mangled hunter bicycle wolf" is pretty darn specific. E-mail requests to the site for sources, clarification or further information went unanswered.

MOVING FORWARD

As a GSE research site, Marysville's full history, landscapes and potential have barely been touched. The options for a serious researcher—beyond merely collecting the reports—are, for all intents and purposes, unlimited. What might be discovered or witnessed should specific sights be targeted with the latest ghost-hunting equipment and techniques?

Do I dare? Will my neighbors show up with a box of chicken feathers and a vat of hot tar?

These sections offer a clear and obvious template for any allowable future action.

Or not.

WHO YA GONNA CALL? GHOSTBUSTERS COME TO TOWN

While I was snooping spooks in Marysville, our local radio station did a Halloween investigation in Helena at an old hospital now renovated as a nursing home. I caught most of news director Troy Shockley and team's report on KCAP's morning *Coffee Break* show. I was busy getting ready for work; it sounded like they got some creepy EVPs, but otherwise I thought it was no comparison to the reports of *this* GSE hot spot in the mountains.

After I dropped a dime, the 2018 *Coffee Break Halloween Special* was scheduled around the first "formal ghosthunter team" to investigate Marysville phantoms. I was to be their guide and host—until the ladies of the two-man and two-woman team turned out to be residents at one time or another, and I became nothing but a tagalong beyond requesting specific sites. It was all I could do to keep up with their self-focused pace. But it allowed me to be in full, open eyes 'n ears witness mode. This gave me a big credibility factor in the end because, unlike my layman suspicions, there was absolutely zero hint of trying to impress me or anybody. Frequently, it was me asking about what got them all excited, looking over their shoulders and so on.

I eventually realized that investigating Marysville had been on their wish list for a while. One lady was with the volunteer fire department, and I overheard her talking about EVPs in the fire station; this was not their first rodeo, nor was I some magical gatekeeper host. They also weren't my employees and in the end walked away with hardcore data (such as vast numbers of words caught on the word generators) that I would have liked. I falsely imagined I could write down the few expected; this was laughable with what turned out to be a flood from multiple devices.

The good news? There is no patience or word count allowance here to accurately describe that fast and furious night down to each relevant detail. It's also good in that I'm still trying to absorb and sort out what happened but had the personal witness to relate what I believe to be the highlights. The *Coffee Break* special had to be broken down into an unprecedented four parts.

SO NOW LET'S CONSIDER what's been learned so far and throw in any revelations from the investigation and where this path we've taken may yet lead.

JULIAN HOUSE

The Julian House and property were sold six months after the poltergeist event. There were no repeat performances in my residence. The only "incident" that could come close to being considered an inexplicable GSE type was a series of three or four sharp, hard knocks one midsummer early evening. They were loud enough to turn my head from the TV and apparently originating in the same hot zone area of the old rooms. Although I was constantly keeping an eye out for any weird happenings, this was dismissed.

Specific reasons included a higher skepticism with bright sun still hanging in the sky and active local wildlife like squirrels and plenty of downy woodpeckers. As I didn't raise my butt from the sofa, there was no investigation past a quick backward glance and shrug. Date and time were not noted. Therefore, it can have no GSE credibility beyond anecdotal.

Considering lots of hours absent from the house, my coma-like sleeping patterns, bilateral myopia and general inattention, Julian House still showed powerful forces and may be much more active than displayed so far; a lot of GSE events may have been missed altogether. That is logical but ultimately speculation. In my opinion (and unless the events that unfolded set things to peace), Julian House is a prime candidate for a total ghost hunter shakedown with every tool in the investigative arsenal.

This is not going to happen anytime soon. The new residents are not enthused about this topic. No one can blame them. They will be left alone to enjoy their home on their own terms, a fundamental right we would all demand in similar circumstances.

I tried two ill-advised walk-bys when the new neighbors had the misfortune to be spotted out in the open in their front yard. That was enough. Yes, they were very polite. No, I sensed zero enthusiasm to embrace wild stories of poltergeists in the kitchen of their new house. History may belong to us all, but nothing else within the boundaries of that now-private property. I have a single good-authority report that "some banging in the kitchen" was heard at some point, yet nevertheless that is just another unsubstantiated rumor. Unless information is volunteered at some point in the future, the story has been told. In fact, the unusual episodic nature of "the haunting" suggests any spirits are now at rest.

It was a perfect plot for a half-hour *Twilight Zone*. "A" leads to "B," which leads to "C" with a good twist at the end (and all due respect for the poor soul). Final words were hidden as mercy to friends and family but were somehow the source for the boy's unsettled spirit to remain earthbound until finally revealed decades later to the surviving sister. The possible significance of the other documents can only be imagined. A 1930s market receipt may rate some mild historical curiosity; it's another thing altogether when it's signed by your grandfather. Returning these into family hands was critical both to this imagined plot line and basic decency.

The utterly freaky retrieval of that 1880s crate panel confirms this was part of whatever GSE forces reside there. How else to explain a deliberate, focused act by myself yet with nothing to do with my brain, conscious control or awareness—to retrieve a specific, extremely relevant target out of a mountain of obscuring clutter? For a few seconds at least, I was an avatar of myself being remotely driven as if through a video game joystick. Imagine patenting such a capability or the NSA getting wind.

Maybe it's a good thing GSEs remain elusive. God willing, there's enough reality to these bizarre events to also believe the process allowed a troubled spirit to move on into peace.

Then it doesn't matter. As we say in the old neighborhood, "That was that. Cue curtain."

Nothing left to see or hear because whatever was behind the GSEs is no longer there. Unless (now cue ominous background music) the poltergeist activity had nothing to do with the mirror lights or vice versa. Or that this did not represent the limits of entity presence. Instinct and the contiguous way multiple events unfolded suggest it was all connected—a singular discrete force that likely no longer manifests.

From a research point, only a few loose ends remain: the exact date, time and site of the past tragedy—brutal inquiries that do not rate infliction on surviving family members. Other records should suffice, and this only to evaluate against the witnessed phenomena. Documentation of the time can provide some startling confirmations, new details that serve as fresh, illuminating puzzle pieces—or offer black-and-white testimony that I'm so off-base I may as well not be in the ballpark.

Obviously, I didn't take the team on *that* porch, no matter how much I wanted. But the disappointment was mitigated when I complained about such and one of the ladies scoffed that she was related to the new owner and current residents were just renters. This suggests the future possibility of real investigation on that site and simmers in the pending file.

In the meantime, "Old Julian House" stands as a peaceful, private-property "New Owners House" off-limits to any further snooping.

THE RED HOUSE

Right track, entirely wrong railroad.

It has turned out that Sherlock had the wrong address. Textbook example of the critical need to gather as many historical data points that may be available—a major problem for Marysville, as discussed below. No wonder that young couple reported nothing but peace. I could have fixed this in pre-editing but feel it's critical to illustrate how GSE investigation facts should be checked and rechecked. I seriously thought I had the right place from several descriptions.

Once cluing in to the truth, the *real* Red House is hard to miss. Vacant for years, it stands in an empty lot on another street, still proudly bearing the faded color of its namesake without apology or deception. Depending on your frame of mind, it's a charming example of late 1800s cottage architecture or the classic site location for a spooky movie. I was allowed a walk-through and found it to be in rather good shape despite some infrastructure damage. Many lives were lived there, and so it felt…almost as if I was an intruding voyeur. Probably was. Standing in the same rooms imagining the previous reports got terrifying fast, an assessment far too unfair with my mindset to document as fact.

That was on a bright summer afternoon. Now I was entering on a cold, drizzly October night. Five other people along helped mitigate the chill. Very creepy staging, but I was downright surprised at the absolute absence of menace or fear. Maybe because of the active team, snapping pictures, setting up remote mics, breaking up into smaller groups and giving the overall impression of walking into a *Ghost Adventures* episode.

I saw word generators on smartphone screens scrolling almost continuously. Medium Michael Sweet seemed to be talking to an unidentified old man spirit connected with farming/ranch terms. One recorder was drained of its battery power seconds after I saw them installed from an unopened package. While I was standing on the stairs, I heard one lady on the lower floor tell her friend she was going out to the truck for fresh batteries after another sudden drain; seconds after her departure, I heard the upstairs group comment on a "VINNIE" term, repeated twice.

Moments later, the other lady came back in, showing her friend the double VINNIE *she* just received after fresh batteries. According to the team, nothing else there repeated twice, much less on separate devices at damn close to the same time. I witnessed it playing out. Oh, and chillingly tempting as it was, I dismiss any personal connection to my own name.

That's because of the most stunning new fact that had just been told to me shortly before: some years ago, Steve Soboyna's daughter did a little hack investigation of her own into the Red House. The highlight were several clear EVPs of repeating *VINNIE*s.

I've since uncovered a lady (data on her, that is) born here in the early 1900s named Vinnie Schafer Kurtz, as well as an entire clan of last-name Vincents. It is now a no-brainer mission to connect the address with the name. Relatives note she grew up in the Historic Shafer House that still survives on another street. Maybe she had a friend here. Nothing obvious arose in connection with the Elegant Lady unless this is Vinnie herself.

This first tour stop wrapped up with a little medium show I will not judge here. I honestly felt a little silly, as this was the first hint of theatrics and I sensed absolutely nothing of what Sweet and others claimed. But then again, that's why they're an investigative team and I'm just recording it. This ring of held hands was preamble to releasing a somewhat sour old man spirit—and the little girl he was keeping with him. Michael and friends called out a great argument for going into the light; it seems the old man wasn't evil, perhaps a relative of the little girl, and was hanging around for all the wrong reasons—reasons that would resolve once he passed into peace. "Your wife is waiting." "You don't want to keep this girl here." A little more heartfelt persuasion, then presto-chango, I'm told the unsettled spirits of the Red House are now at rest. Next?

I shrugged it off at the time, then backtracked and awarded more points on confirming one of the Red House reports I missed. Another trusted neighbor had lived there and was also grateful to leave because of odd phenomena and ghostly glimpses of a spectral little girl and crotchety old man.

There's now hard data that might connect with the site. Standing empty at it is, with extended permission and a bit more courage, this site is prime GSE investigation territory. But if street rumor is to be believed, the clock is ticking: the owners have decided to clear the property of the slowly decaying old building and cart it away for demolition. This could happen next year or next week.

A Morning of Murder and Mayhem

Necessary: confirming the exact location of the Allen residence. Is there any proximity to the empty field off Aspen Way, or is this a separate phenomenon? If the 1896 address in which Wilmot Allen was murdered turns out to be a completely different location across town, then *that* house would be worthwhile to check out if appropriate or even still existent.

Further, what eventually happened to Edith Allen?

UNSETTLED SPIRITS AT MARYSVILLE HOUSE

The team's visit here indicated quite a few spirits indeed, but most were far from "unsettled" and quite content to be haunting the place. According to the dominant spirit of a cheerful female hostess, all is well on the Other Side, they enjoy the atmosphere and the only killjoy is a single male spirit that's "not so bad." She declined an offer to banish him. So reveals Michael Sweet via a disturbing, perfectly timed, one-for-yes, two-for-no interaction between his questions and a beeping EMF (electromagnetic frequency) light sensor sitting by itself in the middle of the dining room

Aspen Way fields where phantom shots heard. *Author photo.*

floor. Word generators come alive; I see STATION pop up after a question about where these spirits reside.

There is no hint or mention of any suicidal stationmasters or negativity in any way. Just the opposite: having been told the story of levitating bottles, Michael asked this lady spirit if she was responsible. I watched a word generator beside me that had lain silent for past minutes pop up a single word: JOKE. "Oh, that was a joke, huh?" *Beep!* YES.

As if that wasn't startling enough, the positive attention allowed bartender Chris Boyles to come forward and officially testify to the shocking experience of levitating bottles as previously told. Yet even this had its odd moments. KCAP news director Troy Shockley sat down in the dining room for the formal interview. Then a bizarre, never-before digital recorder malfunction: despite seeing the screen dutifully displaying the flowing spikes of their voice waveforms, the playback reproduced Chris and background loud and clear—but none of Troy's questions were recorded.

A last confirmation came with the sensitive members of the team noticing a heavy presence around the same dining room storeroom employees have previously felt themselves. There was nothing specific except rare glimpsed shadows and a certainty of *something* askew. Only days later, staff reported a woman customer (and sensitive herself in some manner) felt a powerful presence in the same location. She claimed to have clearly received the name JOCELYN—another gold nugget of hard data if it can be associated with the location.

CHINESE DISTRICT

Chinese immigrants were a big part of Marysville's history. Along with their merchant shops and laundries, many of their homes were clustered around the steep hillsides around Picnic Hill and adjacent land next to Grand Street. Excavations during road improvement resulted in the discovery of the largest collection of pioneer Chinese artifacts in the state. The area is all open field and tumbled stone foundations now. It was not on my list this cold, rainy night, but the team had other ideas, and I found myself tromping through a wet field while Michael Sweet described large crowds of Chinese spirits. Not all were very happy. TAXES, UNFAIR and other like terms showed on the generators.

I had explored these scattered foundation ruins many times myself and still felt nothing but awe at what it took to live up here during past times. Completing my circuit of the field and gaining nothing but wet socks, I ended up beside Michael. He was holding out his smartphone word generator, not getting any activity at the moment. Credibility of these devices remains up in the air; I mean, how exactly do they do their job? Do ghosts have keyboards? They somehow sense phantom thoughts? Does anyone care to describe the programming on that, because it'd be real neat to operate our smartphones just by thinking at 'em. Such was my state of mind when I asked how accurate those things were. "Do you think they detect the general sense of things, or can they be specific?"

Beep! Sweet just shrugged and showed me the screen: AUTHOR. "You tell me." His fingers never moved from their casual grip on the device.

It was an interesting and humbling complimentary recognition but would have had more authority if it declared the day-to-day reality of COMMERCIAL PAINTER and WALLPAPERER. And yes, things had progressed to real book research, but how did the Chinese spirits know that? I suppose by then I had exposed my plans and they either were following me around or heard through the phantom grapevine. It's intriguing and unsettling to think I'm being watched in real time.

OTHERS

The last stop was an excursion to the cemetery a mile above town. There was no more drizzle, but it was cloudy and pitch dark—every bit as spooky as I had imagined after several times chickening out to visit at night. Again, the lively company—as well as a couple of interested bar patrons—banished anxiety and turned the eerie set into an adventure—a rather dull one in the end.

I agree with Michael Sweet's explanation: he and other mediums believe graveyards are the polar opposite of their erroneous reputation. Spirits may exist there, but the vast majority soon move on to places more meaningful to them. "Hanging around a boneyard is boring," he says. Neither he nor any of the other sensitives reported a thing. There was nothing on the cameras. They were all negative except for two other strange disruptions of Troy Shockley's recorder. In two locations, it picked up a disturbing hiss or scrap of hostile speech that could very well be accepted as muffled, as if from coming underground.

It is hoped that further analysis of this investigation connects to some hard evidence.

The same general need to dig deeper applies to the rest of the reports and locations. Some of those random stories from the far past may become big ones in the present if exact locations are determined and then followed up with serious methodology and equipment. Dark Cabin obviously looms above them all. Is this case completely out of our league, better left alone or both? The latest story to arise concerns a freakin' *magician* who had once lived there, toying with ill-advised powers that only made things worse. My preferred strategy has evolved to respectfully ignore it at the time being because there are plenty of other distractions. Further investigations of the reports thus far may deliver results that would make avoiding Dark Cabin a no-brainer or suggest that it be left to professional ghost hunters, if there is such a thing.

Note I didn't ask for this topic. I had no idea I'd landed in GSE Central.

Of one thing I'm certain: there are many more GSE reports and events yet to be revealed.

TREASURE MAPS BY ANY DEFINITION

It's too bad a pair of the best tools for historical research remain missing. As of 2018, the most critical resources that yet elude modern discovery are two Marysville "treasure maps" that represent a pair of Holy Grails for everybody from historical researchers, local families and the Pioneer Society to GSE hunters: a city directory and cemetery plot map.

To be fair with what I've heard, Marysville *is thought* never to have had a city directory—the frontier version of a phone book listing names, occupations, ads and vital exact street addresses. But this is from random inquiries that, from much personal experience, may have been misunderstood. Nobody else has since claimed its existence. Yet it seems unlikely such a bustling metropolis would never have produced a directory of some kind. The truth may simply be that nothing of the like has survived. A lot of items got torched in the devastating fire of 1910. There are many subset listings from local cities, but they do not include street addresses and are limited in extent.

Having a list of historic addresses would be key to matching specific events (such as the Allen killings) to specific places (the empty field with its phantom gunshots). It would prove to be an invaluable guide in many other

Aftermath of the 1910 fire. *Marysville Pioneer Society.*

Fire wasteland as depicted in a Charles Dudley postcard. (As well as postmaster duties, Dudley operated a drugstore.) *Marysville Pioneer Society.*

After the fire, 1910 landscape. *Marysville Pioneer Society.*

ways. A lot of anonymous shacks, cabins and ruined homes would regain their names and history.

The Marysville Cemetery is falling into an overgrown ruin. Only a fraction of markers survive, perhaps a dozen larger stone monuments and tombstones amid an uncounted multitude of long-forgotten unmarked graves. I have heard of plans to use a metal detector in hopes of identifying small clusters of rust occurring along straight-line vectors—the remnants of nails used to hold long-eroded wooden crosses together and thus defining the location of grave rows. A recent recruitment of rescue dogs helped last year to identify a few graves. Most of the sloping mountain property northeast of town is buried in years' accumulation of dead grasses and a Devil's Golf Course of weed humps, gopher tunnels and a weird chaotic selection of shallow craters needing refill each spring and marking, I assume, collapsed coffins below ground.

Many of the pioneers, family members and subjects of these reports have been laid to rest in this cemetery. But exactly where? Nobody knows today. No complete census, plot map or layout diagram can be found. However, there's a tantalizing hope that just such a key location map does exist. One resident "swears" he saw one somewhere down the line, years ago. That may not be encouraging for lost car keys, but this is a credible report from a credible witness that he had eyes on a surviving map this side of the twenty-first century.

Got anything in *your* attic?

The search goes on.

BIBLIOGRAPHY

Anker, Conrad, and David Roberts. *The Lost Explorer: Finding Mallory on Mount Everest*. New York: Simon and Schuster, 1999.

Asimov, Isaac. *Asimov's Biographical Encyclopedia of Science and Technology*. 2nd revised ed. Garden City, NY: Doubleday and Company, Inc., 1982.

Ayres, Thomas. *A Military Miscellany*. Stirling Edition. New York: Bantam Books, 2006.

Baker, Alan. *Ghosts and Spirits*. New York: Orion Media, TV Books, LLC, 1998.

Barrell, Joseph. *Geology of the Marysville Mining District, Montana: A Study of Igneous Intrusion and Contact Metamorphism*. U.S. Deparment of the Interior, United States Geological Survey. Washington, D.C.: Government Printing Office, 1907.

Burland, C.A. *Beyond Science: A Journey into the Supernatural*. New York: Grossett and Dunlap, Inc., 1972.

Caras, Roger A. *Dangerous to Man: The Definitive Story of Wildlife's Reputed Dangers*. Revised ed. New York: Holt, Rinehart and Winston of Canada, Ltd., 1975.

Collier, Graham, and Patricia Collier. *Antarctic Odyssey: In the Footsteps of the South Polar Explorers*. New York: Carroll and Graf Publishers, 1999.

Davis, Wade. *Into the Silence: The Great War, Mallory, and the Conquest of Everest*. New York: Vintage Books, 2012.

Fred, Earl. *Marysville, It's* [sic] *History and It's* [sic] *People*. Helena, MT: Earl Fred, 2013.

Ghost Adventures. DVD documentary. Zak Bagans, Aaron Goodwin and Nick Groff. 4Reel Productions, LLC. 87 mins. From *Ghost Encounters* DVD bundled w/2 other unrelated features. 2011 Echo Bridge Home Entertainment.

Guralnik, David B., ed. *Webster's New World Dictionary of the American Language*. 2nd College Edition. Cleveland, OH: William Collins Publishers, Inc., 1979.

Into the Unknown. N.p.: Reader's Digest Association, Inc., 1981.

Jackson, Joe. *Atlantic Fever: Lindbergh, His Competitors, and the Race to Cross the Atlantic*. New York: Picador, 2012.

Langer, William L. *An Encyclopedia of World History*. 5th ed. Boston: Houghton Mifflin Company, 1972.

Lansing, Alfred. *Endurance: Shackelton's Incredible Voyage*. 1959. Repr., New York: Basic Books, 2007.

Man, Myth & Magic: An Illustrated Encyclopedia of the Supernatural. Vol. 4, *Celts to Cult of the Dead*; vol. 15, *New Religious Movements—Palm*. Edited by Richard Cavendish. New York: BPC Publishing, 1970.

Matthews, Rupert. *Sasquatch: True Life Encounters with Legendary Ape-Men*. Edison, NJ: Chartwell Books, Inc., 2008.

Melton, Marilyn. Letter to author describing bear encounter. 2016.

Moravek, Vincent A. *It Happened in Glacier National Park*. 2nd ed. Guilford, CT: Globe Pequot Press, 2013.

Mysteries of the Unknown (series). *Hauntings, Phantom Encounters, Mystic Places* and *Psychic Voyages*. New York: Time-Life Books Inc., 1989.

Nature's Extremes: Earthquakes, Tsunamis and Other Natural Disasters that Shape Life on Earth. New York: Time Home, n.d.

Out of This World: The Illustrated Library of the Bizarre and Extraordinary. Vol. 1. New York: Phoebus Publishing Company, 1978.

Quest for the Unknown: Ghosts and Hauntings. Pleasantville, NY: Reader's Digest Association, Inc., 1991.

Quest for the Unknown: Unsolved Mysteries of the Past. Pleasantville, NY: Reader's Digest Association, Inc., 1993.

Rosenberg, Donna. *World Mythology: An Anthology of Great Myths and Epics*. Chicago: National Textbook Company, 1988.

Steedman, Scott. *Ancient Egypt*. American ed. New York: Dorling Kindersley Publishing, 1995.

Strange but True (magazine). Vol. 8, no. 9, November 10, 2008.

Strange Stories, Amazing Facts: Stories that Are Bizarre, Unusual, Odd, Astonishing and Often Incredible. Pleasantville, NY: Reader's Digest Association, Inc., 1977.

Swallow, G.C. *Reports of the Inspectors of Mines and Deputy Inspectors of Mines for the Year Ending November 30th, 1890*. N.p., 1891.

Waite, Susan. *An Historical Inventory of the Marysville Ghost Town*. Missoula, MT: Bureau of Land Management, [1971].

Warren, Joshua P. *How to Hunt Ghosts: A Practical Guide*. New York: Fireside, 2003.

Wilson, Colin. *Enigmas and Mysteries*. London: Aldus Books Limited, 1976.

Wood, Gerald L. *Animal Facts and Feats*. N.p.: Guinness Superlatives, Ltd., 1972.

Zubrin, Robert, with Richard Wagner. *The Case for Mars: The Plan to Settle the Red Planet and Why We Must*. New York: Simon and Schuster, 1997.

About the Author

After twenty years working in acute medical care, Vince Moravek escaped humid climes and steady employment for the wonders of Montana as a freelance writer, artist and cartoonist (latter most known for the five-year run of *Zink* in Helena's *Queen City News*). Since he became an accidental resident of Marysville in 2016, he has run the Snowline History Museum, established the *Marysville Dispatch* as a modest resurrection of the newspapers of old and is involved in local historic preservation efforts.

Visit us at
www.historypress.com